PONTYPRIDD TO MERTHYR

Vic Mitchell and Keith Smith

Front cover: No. 47257 **Black Lion** *was recorded near Merthyr Vale on 20th July 1978. There were insufficient DMUs to work all the trains at peak hours at this period. (P.Jones)*

Back cover upper: Creeping over the Brunel designed wooden viaduct in the Dare Valley is an excursion train from Cwmaman, which is running towards Gelli Tarw Junction from Dare Junction. The picture is probably from the 1930s; the route closed in 1939. The TVR Dare Valley branch passed under this viaduct. (R.Marrows/S.Vincent coll.)

Back cover lower: At work in the Merthyr Vale Colliery on 26th August 1970 is ex-GWR 0-6-0PT no. 9600. It worked here until 1973 and was subsequently preserved at Tyseley. In the background is an Andrew Barclay 0-6-0T. (A.C.Hartless)

Published February 2012

ISBN 978 1 908174 14 7

© Middleton Press, 2012

Design Deborah Esher

Published by
    Middleton Press
    Easebourne Lane
    Midhurst
    West Sussex
    GU29 9AZ
Tel: 01730 813169
Fax: 01730 812601
Email: info@middletonpress.co.uk
www.middletonpress.co.uk

Printed in the United Kingdom by Henry Ling Limited, at the Dorset Press, Dorchester, DT1 1HD

CONTENTS

1. Pontypridd to Merthyr — 1-53
2. Nelson Branch — 54-60
3. Ynysybwl Branch — 61-69
4. Quakers Yard to Merthyr — 70-77
5. Dare & Aman Branch — 78-81
6. Aberdare Branch — 82-120

INDEX

- 110 Aberaman
- 77 Abercanaid
- 106 Abercwmboi Halt
- 15 Abercynon
- 82 Abercynon North
- 120 Aberdare
- 114 Aberdare Low Level
- 75 Aberfan
- 54 Berw Road Halt
- 79 Black Lion Crossing Halt
- 55 Cilfynydd
- 61 Clydach Court Halt
- 80 Cwmaman Colliery Halt
- 112 Cwmbach
- 109 Fernhill
- 88 Matthewstown Halt
- 48 Merthyr
- 33 Merthyr Vale
- 102 Mountain Ash
- 96 Mountain Ash (Oxford St)
- 59 Nelson (Glam)
- 69 Old Ynysybwl Halt
- 89 Penrhiwceiber Low Level
- 39 Pentre-Bach
- 84 Pontcynon Halt
- 1 Pontypridd
- 30 Quakers Yard
- 70 Quakers Yard High Level
- 25 Quakers Yard Low Level
- 63 Robertstown Halt
- 58 Travellers Rest Halt
- 37 Troed-y-rhiw
- 65 Ynysybwl
- 62 Ynysybwl (New Road) Halt

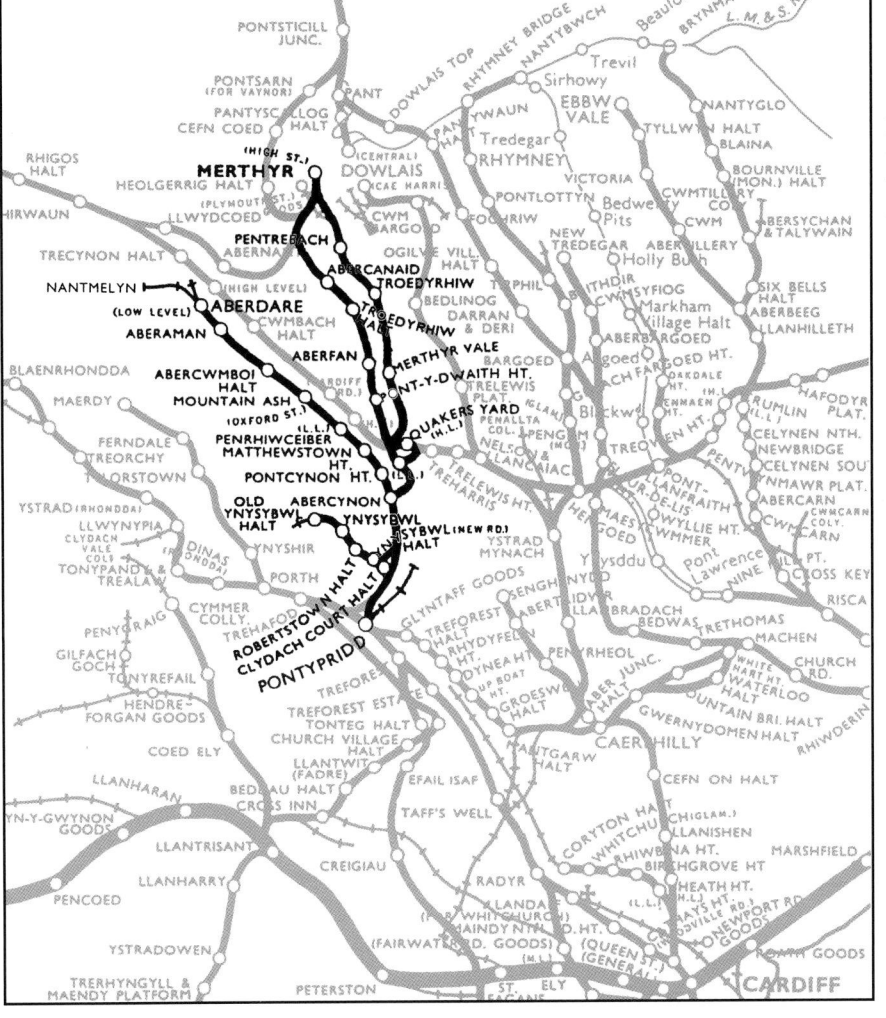

I. GWR map for 1947, with the routes in this album bold.

ACKNOWLEDGEMENTS

We are very grateful for the assistance received from many of those mentioned in the credits also to B.Bennett, B.W.L.Brooksbank, A.R.Carder, R.Caston, G.Croughton, M.J.Furnell, S.C.Jenkins, M.A.N.Johnston, C.G.Maggs, N.Langridge, B.I.Nathan, Mr D. and Dr S.Salter, N.Spilsbury, N.W.Sprinks, M.J.Stretton, T.Walsh and in particular, our always supportive wives, Barbara Mitchell and Janet Smith.

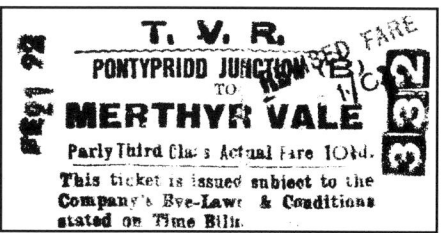
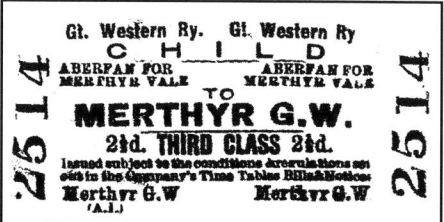

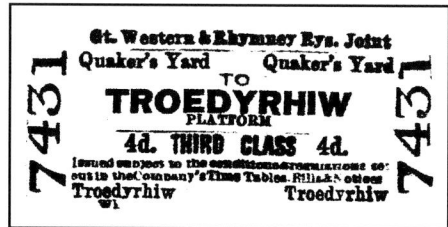

GEOGRAPHICAL SETTING

Pontypridd is at the confluence of the east flowing Afon Rhondda with the south flowing River Taff. About one mile north up the Taff Vale, the Nant Clydach flows in from the west from Ynysybwl. A further mile or more and the Afon Cynon flows in from the northwest at Abercynon, this being close to the branch all the way to Aberdare.

The Taff Vale continues north, steadily becoming narrower, the River Taff eventually flowing along the western flank of Merthyr Tydfil. This large and old established industrial town originally had the benefits of both coal and iron ore being near the surface. It is situated at the foot of the Brecon Beacons and an east-west outcrop of limestone proved to be of value for producing the flux needed in the smelting of the iron. Thus the stage was set for a massive industrial development, which badly scarred the environment, until recent times. The coal basin dips steeply south of the town and thus most of the coal mines featured in this album were very deep. There were more than 70 in the Cynon Valley alone by 1856.

The maps are to the scale of 25ins to 1 mile, with north at the top, unless otherwise indicated. Welsh spelling and hyphenation has varied over the years and so we have generally used the form of the period.

HISTORICAL BACKGROUND

The Taff Vale Railway opened between Cardiff and Abercynon (called Navigation House initially) on 9th October 1840 and here it met the 4ft 4ins gauge Merthyr Tramroad, which had become a world first with steam traction from 21st February 1804. A new line was constructed from Abercynon to Merthyr (Plymouth Street) and the TVR operated passenger trains over it from 21st April 1841, abandoning a rope worked incline in 1867. A branch ran west from Pontypridd into the Rhondda Valley from 1841 and east to Llancaiach from the same year. The Aberdare Railway operated between Abercynon and Aberdare from 6th August 1846, being taken over by the TVR on 1st January 1847.

Merthyr High Street had first been reached by the Vale of Neath Railway's branch through Merthyr Tunnel from the west at Gelli Tarw Junction in November 1853. A short branch to Ynysybwl opened in 1886 and had a passenger service from 1st January 1890 until 28th July 1952.

The TVR became part of the Great Western Railway in 1922, this company having operated between Aberdare and Quakers Yard since 1864 (Neath from 1863). It also ran to Merthyr from Quakers Yard jointly with the Rhymney Railway. This route was in use from 1st April 1886, but was closed suddenly on 3rd February 1951, due to an unsafe viaduct.

The TVR began to run between Pontypridd and Nelson on 25th November 1842 and a passenger service was started on 1st June 1900, but it ceased on 12th September 1932. Merthyr had been reached by the Brecon & Merthyr Railway in 1867. Trains from England on the London & North Western route (originally a Newport, Abergavenny & Hereford Railway branch) came from Abergavenny from 1873 until 1958. The GWR carried passengers to Cwmaman from 1st January 1906, but the service ceased on 22nd September 1924. It was known as the Dare & Aman branch.

The GWR formed the Western Region of British Railways upon nationalisation in 1948 and passenger services were lost between Abercynon and Aberdare on 16th March 1964. Details of withdrawals of freight services are given in the captions. Most services were diesel operated from 13th January 1958.

Privatisation in 1996 resulted in South Wales & West providing services ("South" was dropped in 1998). However, after reorganisation in 2001, Wales & Borders became the franchisee and Arriva Trains Wales took over in December 2003.

The former TVR main line and its branch from Pontypridd to the Rhondda Valley are still both busy, as is the branch to Aberdare. The latter reopened on 3rd October 1988, although the western end had by then been diverted onto the original GWR route.

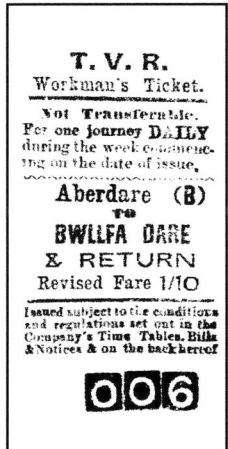 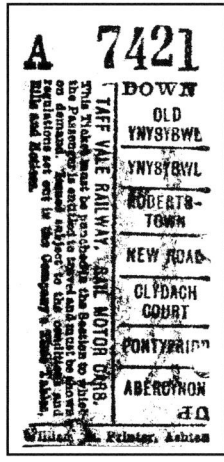

PASSENGER SERVICES

Pontypridd to Merthyr

The table below indicates the train frequency over the route on at least five days per week.

	Weekdays	Sundays
1841	4	0
1850	3	2
1869	4	2
1895	15	2
1921	26	4
1950	37	9
1983	15	7
2011	30	7

Nelson Branch

This carried six or seven trains, weekdays only, throughout its short life.

Ynysybwl Branch

The 1890 timetable showed two trains each weekday, with three extras on Wednesdays and four more on Saturdays. The service in 1920 offered 12 weekday trains, with 2 extra on Saturdays. In 1952, the figures were 5 and 3.

Dare & Aman Branch

In 1907, there were 8 weekday trains, with 5 extras on Saturdays. The figures in 1923 were 10 and 2.

Quakers Yard to Merthyr

The initial timetables showed four weekday and two Sunday trains. By 1914, the figures were 14 and 2. The 1934 service comprised 8 trains on weekdays, but none on Sundays. In the final full year, there were seven trains, weekdays only.

Aberdare Branch

In addition to the trains listed in the table, there were railmotors operating between Abercynon and Aberdare (Mill Street) from 20th December 1904, these calling also at the intermediate platforms, as the TVR described the halts. Initially there were six trips each way, with five more on Saturday evenings, but none on Sundays. The two platforms north of Aberdare station were not used by the public after 1st June 1912.

	Weekdays	Sundays
1850	3	2
1880	5	2
1920	12	4
1950	19	9
1964	9	0

From October 1988, the trains ran once every two hours Mondays to Fridays, hourly on Saturdays, with none on Sundays. By 2001, the service was hourly throughout the week. By 2005, it had a 30-minute operation on weekdays, for most of the day.

August 1892

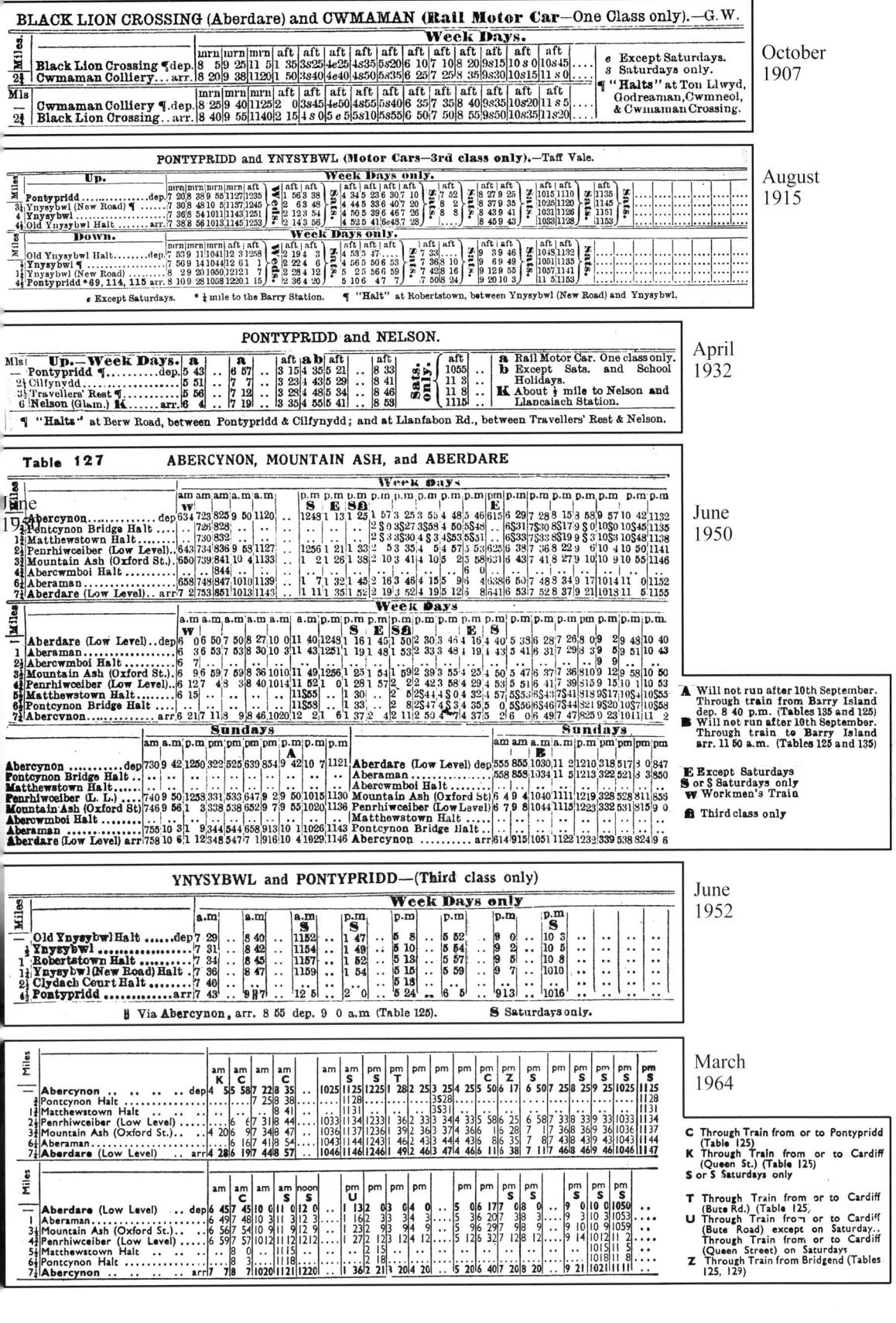

1. Pontypridd to Merthyr
PONTYPRIDD

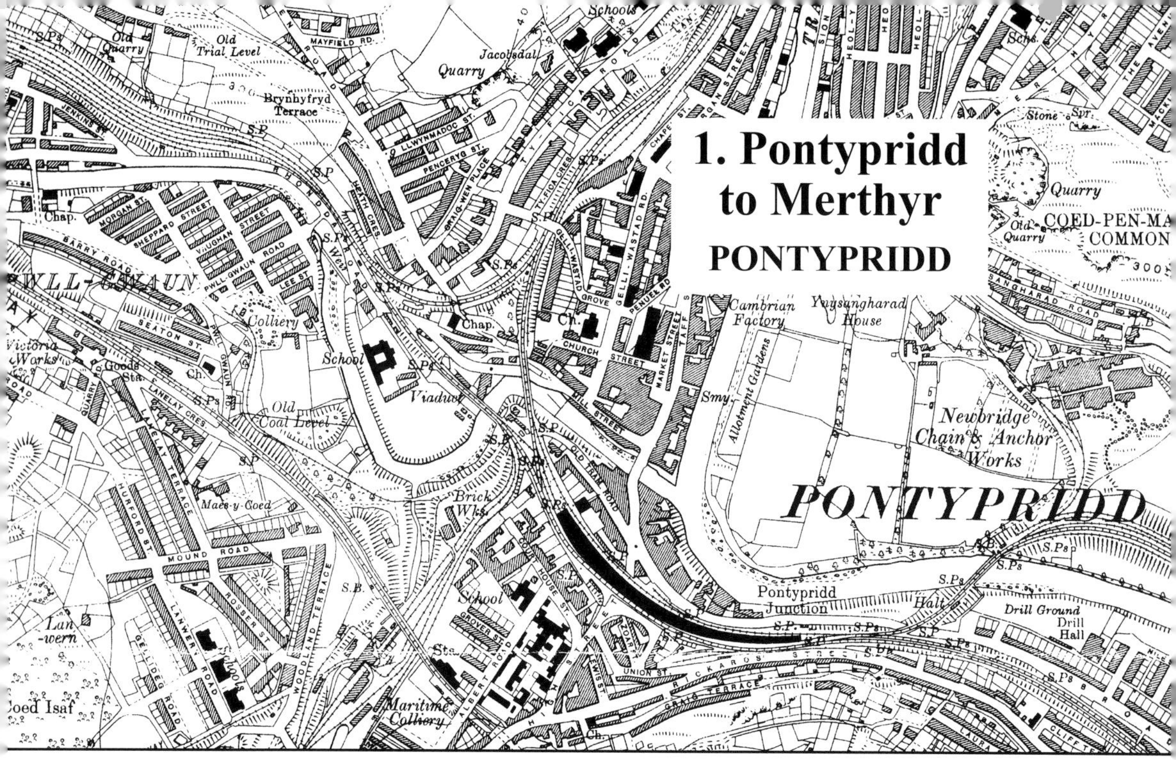

II.   The 1921 edition at 6ins to 1 mile has the TVR from Cardiff to Merthyr from lower right to top centre. Joining from the right is the 1884 line from Caerphilly, but trains from there terminated at Tram Road halt, between the junction and the bridge over the Taff, until 1922. The wide black curve represents the extensive station roof and at its north end is the 1872 triangular junction with the TVRs main line to the Rhondda, which runs to the top left of the map. Running diagonally below it is the Barry Railway, its station (called Graig) being shown near Maritime Colliery.

1.   The final rebuild resulted in two long through platforms - No. 1 and No. 6. We are between bay platforms No. 3 and No. 4 and are looking north in about 1925, with the Merthyr lines curving right and the 1902 Junction Box centre. It was in use until 15th October 1998. (R.M.Casserley coll.)

2. Northbound on 11th September 1951 is no. 344, an ex-TVR 0-6-2T. It is standing at platform No. 2, which was inset into No. 1 at its north end. No. 7 was inset into No. 6 at the south of the station and was the final bay in use, lasting until 1980. (H.C.Casserley)

III. The full extent of the platform roof is revealed on the 1922 map and the lengthy canopy over the entrance is shown with diamonds. The confluence of the Taff and the Rhondda is top centre. The first station was of Brunel's Chalet style and was called Newbridge initially. Junction was added in about 1862 and it became Pontypridd in 1902. The suffix Central was applied in 1922-30. The first structure lasted until 1891; the present one was created in 1906-07, but a new entrance was provided in 1976.

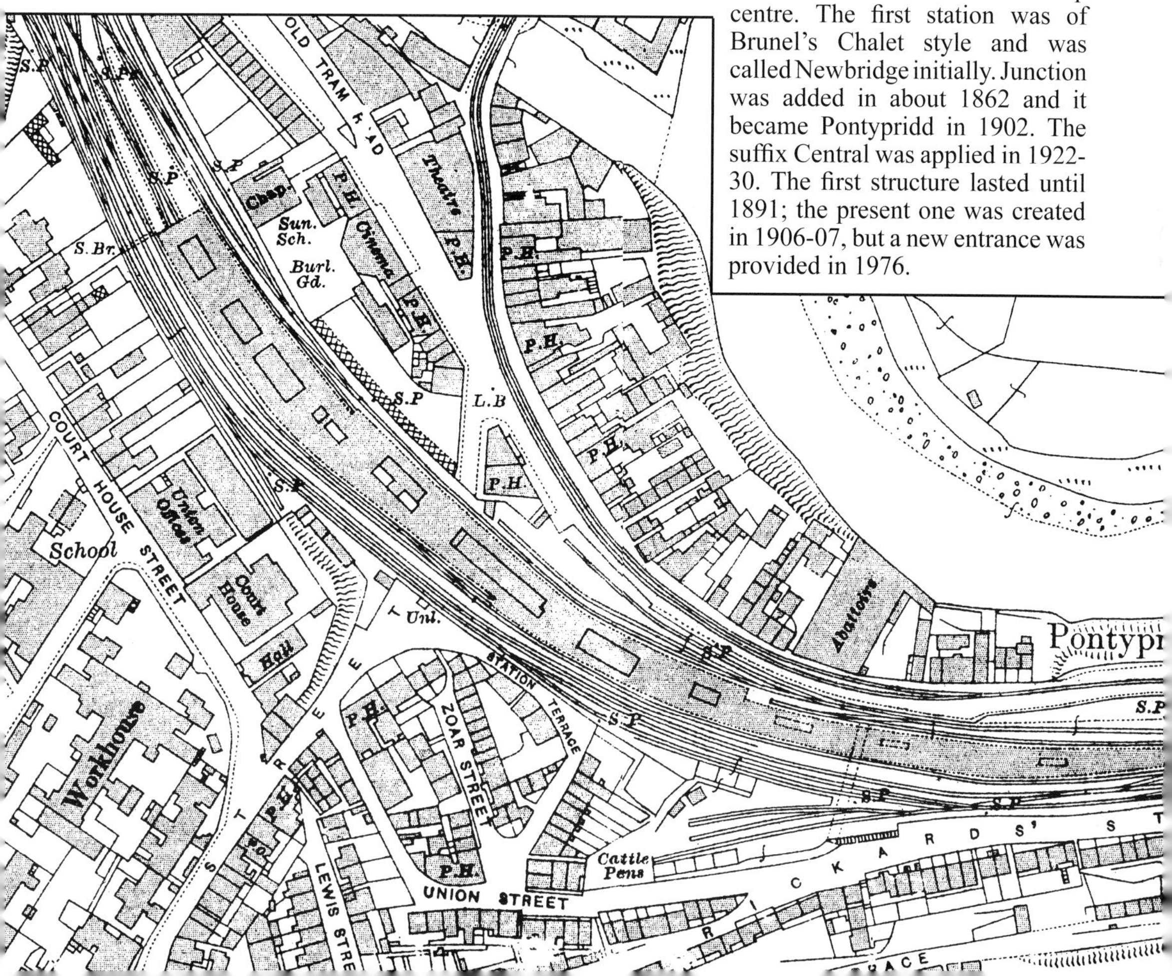

3.   At platform 2 on 9th June 1957 is 0-6-0PT no. 6417 with a train for Aberdare. Alterations in 1969-70 resulted in No. 1 being the only through platform and most of the bays were lost. However, a new through platform, west of No. 1, came into use on 16th September 1991 and became No. 2. (Colour-Rail.com)

4.   The 1991 platform is on the left in this northward view from 13th February 2009 and a train is signalled for the Treherbert route. The other line is reversible and serves platform No. 1. On the right is the former No. 2, which includes a sign for the Chaplains Office. No. 1 takes 12 coaches and No. 2 had been extended to take six. (V.Mitchell)

5. The 1976 entrance is pictured on the same day. It is much further north than its predecessor, which was close to the road bridge shown on the map. The style of glazing was subsequently changed dramatically. (V.Mitchell)

Other views of this station and junction can be seen in *Cardiff to Pontypridd* and *Pontypridd to Port Talbot*.

6. The rear of the 13.50 Merthyr to Barry Island is on Merthyr Viaduct on 24th March 1976 and the front of it is close to Junction Box, which had 135 levers at its maximum and closed in 1998. (T.Heavyside)

7. A little further north, 60 minutes earlier, we have evidence that the route was initially single track. The old arches are over the Afon Cynon and the new span is over the circulatory system. (T.Heavyside)

8. A view south from Thomas Street bridge (centre of map IV) in 1922 has the 1872 curve on the right and the line from Pontypridd on the left. The curve was used mainly for freight and closed on 4th August 1968. Pontypridd Northern Junction Box had 34 levers and was in use from 1888 until 21st August 1951. (D.K.Jones coll.)

9. A Merthyr to Cardiff DMU runs close to the very extensive goods yard on 10th February 1978, three years before its closure. (P.Jones)

10. Pont Shon Norton Box was photographed from the south on 5th June 1960. It had 60 levers and closed on 13th January 1970. It was at the 1887 junction for the Pont Shon Norton branch, which is lower right on the next map. The line is in the foreground and it passes behind the box and then to the right of the white building in the distance. (M.Dart/Transport Treasury)

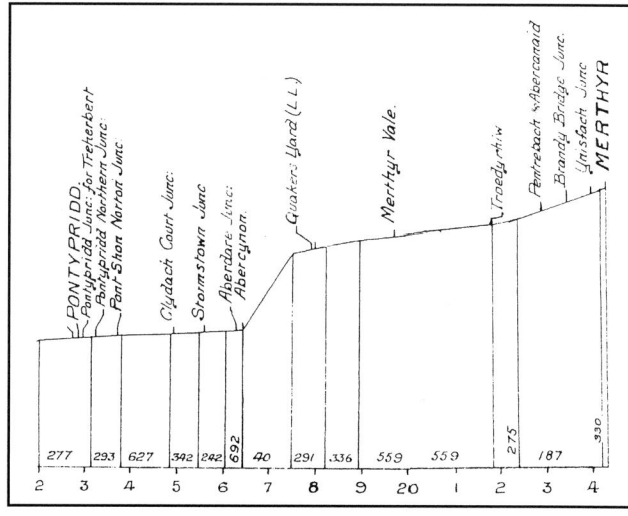

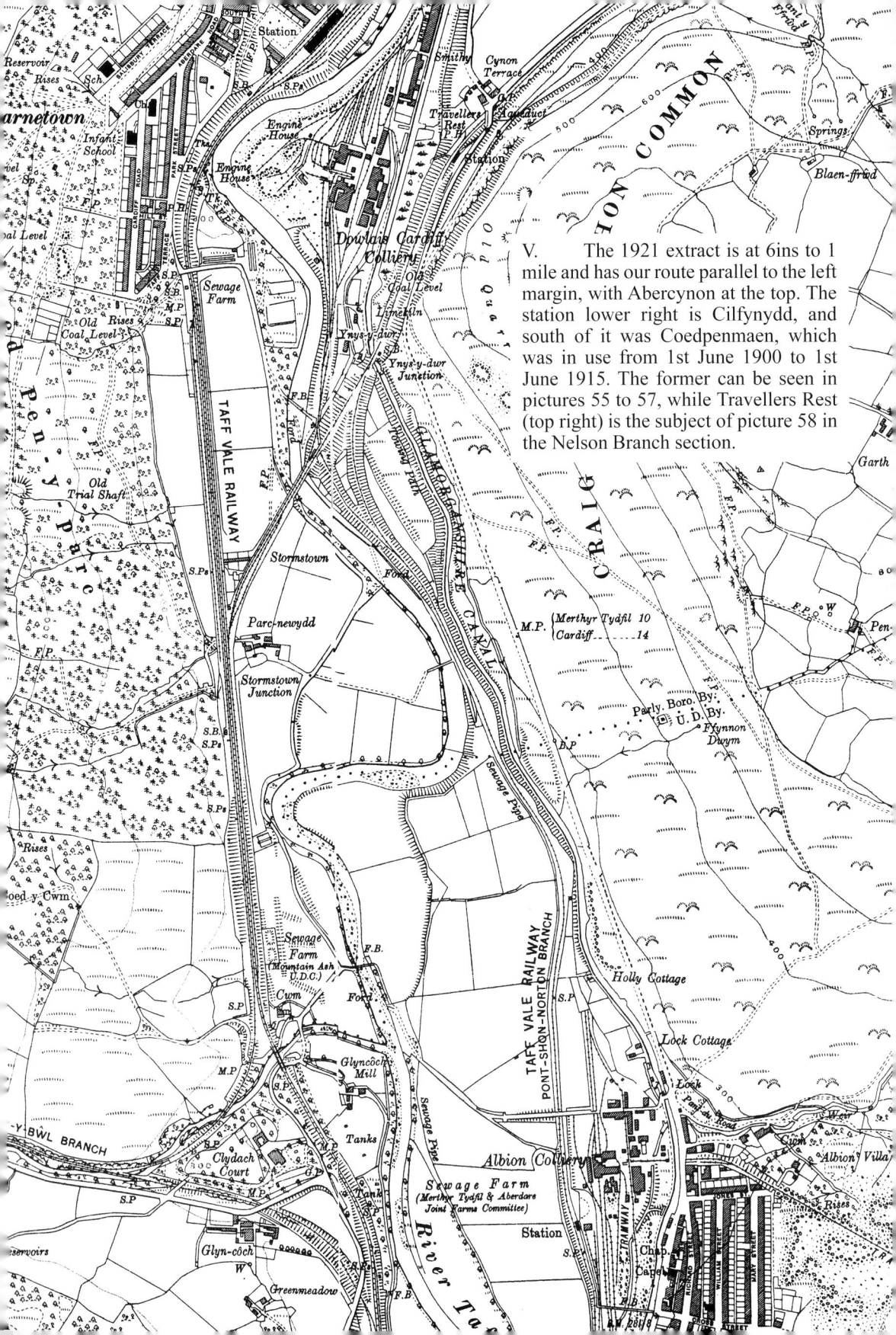

V. The 1921 extract is at 6ins to 1 mile and has our route parallel to the left margin, with Abercynon at the top. The station lower right is Cilfynydd, and south of it was Coedpenmaen, which was in use from 1st June 1900 to 1st June 1915. The former can be seen in pictures 55 to 57, while Travellers Rest (top right) is the subject of picture 58 in the Nelson Branch section.

11. The next box to the north was Clydach Court Junction, where the Ynysybwl Branch diverged west. The box was built in 1940 following a fire. It housed 46 levers and lasted until 6th November 1962. The junction is lower left on map V. Northbound on 5th November 1958 is 0-6-2T no. 5644 with a train from Coke Ovens. (S.Rickard/J&J coll.)

12. This is the 1841 junction for the Nelson Branch and is seen from the south on 5th June 1960. It is halfway up the left side of the map and marked as Stormstown Junction. The 80-lever box also controlled the northern apex of the triangular junction with the Ynysybwl branch. Closure came on 4th September 1977. (M.Dart/Transport Treasury)

13. Freight loops were provided at Stormstown and no. 37271 is running round its train from Lady Windsor Colliery on 24th September 1980. This opened in 1886 and closed in 1988. (D.H.Mitchell)

14. Carn Park box was the next one north and it is seen on 12th January 1960, as 0-6-2T no. 5601 approaches. The 42-lever frame was in use until 31st July 1966. Its smoke obscures a NCB small coal stack siding, which supplied material to Aberthaw Power Station in the 1970s. It was capable of burning fine coal dust, including river dredgings. (S.Rickard/J&J coll.)

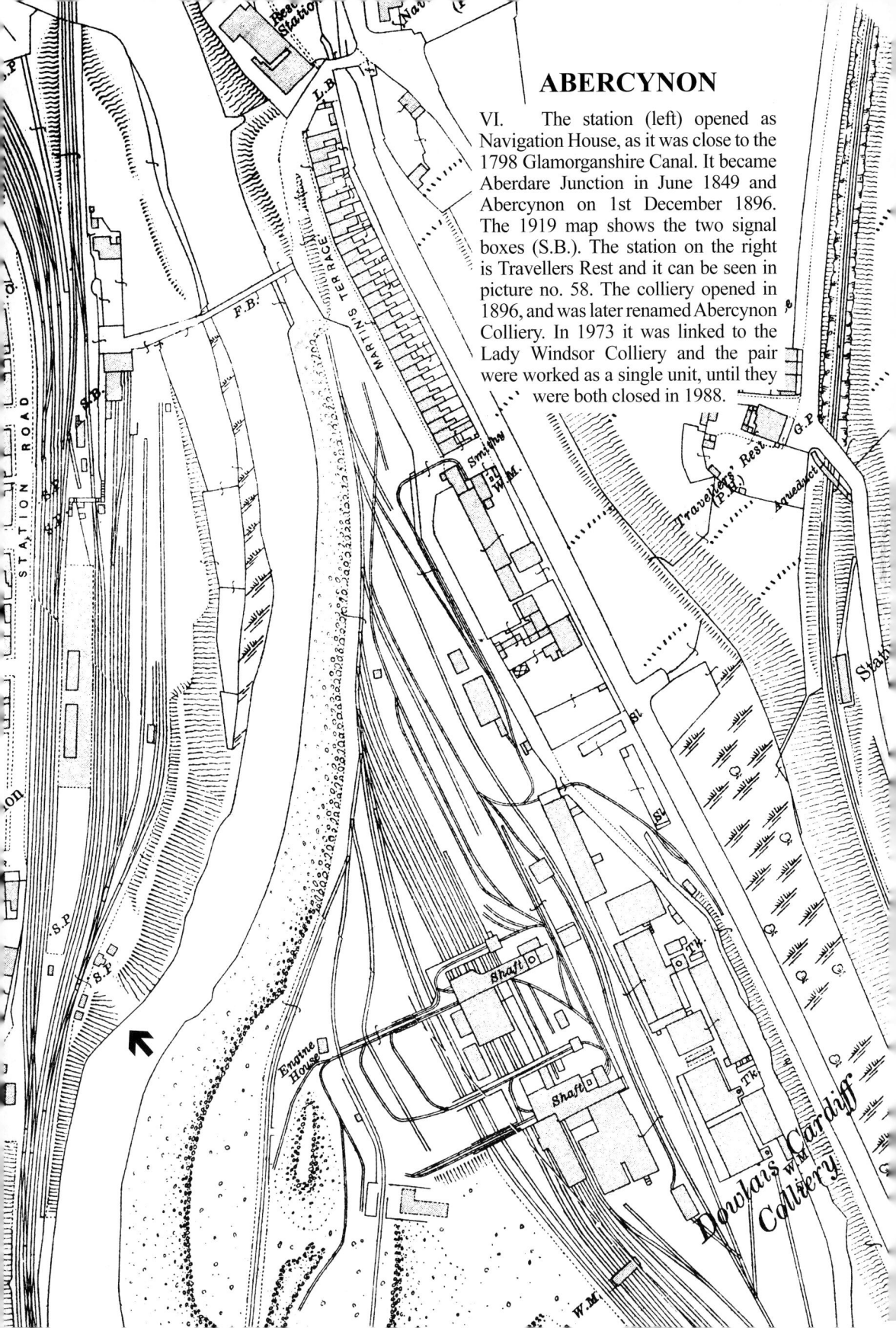

ABERCYNON

VI. The station (left) opened as Navigation House, as it was close to the 1798 Glamorganshire Canal. It became Aberdare Junction in June 1849 and Abercynon on 1st December 1896. The 1919 map shows the two signal boxes (S.B.). The station on the right is Travellers Rest and it can be seen in picture no. 58. The colliery opened in 1896, and was later renamed Abercynon Colliery. In 1973 it was linked to the Lady Windsor Colliery and the pair were worked as a single unit, until they were both closed in 1988.

15. An early postcard includes the first engine shed, on the right. The footbridge is in the distance in this northward view. The staff of 86 listed in 1923 included train crew. The figure was down to 62 by 1934. (Lens of Sutton coll.)

16. The coal stage was an unusual subject for a postcard. "Wish you were here" would apply to those specifically interested in three-plank wagons dedicated to locomotive coal.
(Lens of Sutton coll.)

Abercynon	1923	1933
Passenger tickets issued	120238	43998
Season tickets issued	746	364
Parcels forwarded	22697	22462
General goods forwarded (tons)	452	313
Coal and coke received (tons)	186	1461
Other minerals received (tons)	10792	3314
General goods received (tons)	29381	23038
Coal and Coke handled	491784	491951
Trucks of livestock handled	132	63

17. The first engine shed opened in 1853 and lasted until 1928. This one was in use from 1929 until 2nd November 1964 and is seen in 1938. (D.K.Jones coll.)

18. The coal stage seen in picture 16 was devoid of a shelter and was replaced by the standard GWR design, with a water tank on top and an incline for wagons to be propelled up to the first floor. Seen on 13th July 1958 is 0-6-0PT no. 4626. (H.C.Casserley)

19.   The 11.00am autotrain from Aberdare Low Level is arriving on 3rd August 1957, with 0-6-0PT no. 6431 between two of the coaches. (S.Rickard/J&J coll.)

20.   It is 17th August 1963 and a DMU waits to leave for Cardiff. The signal box had 93 levers, but these were reduced to 35 by about 1971. The box had been at Birmingham Moor Street and Didcot Foxhall Junction prior to coming into use here on 3rd April 1932. (P.J.Garland/R.S.Carpenter)

21.	This northward view from August 1963 still has double track to both Merthyr (right) and Aberdare (left). The latter lost its passenger service on 16th March 1964. (P.J.Garland/R.S.Carpenter)

22.	A panorama from 26th March 1976 has no. 37281 working south on the remaining Aberdare line, while the locomotive depot site was in commercial use. Its coding had been 86J until January 1961, when it became 88J. The signal box had the lower timber part replaced by brickwork in 1977. It was closed in 2008 and replaced by a Portakabin. (T.Heavyside)

23. The 10.49 Merthyr to Penarth is arriving on 30th April 1985. The double track southward then began behind the camera. When the Aberdare service was resumed on 3rd October 1988, a platform was opened on the inside of the curve on the left and it was known as Abercynon North (see pictures 82-83). The original island platform then became South. (A.C.Hartless)

24. Both faces of the original island platform were back in use from 18th May 2008, a subway having been built and new connections having been laid to both routes, north of the station. This is the 11.38 from Merthyr on 13th February 2009 and snow was threatened. (V.Mitchell)

**QUAKERS YARD
LOW LEVEL**

25. A westward panorama from the footbridge on 1st August 1956 features the 35-lever signal box, which was in use until 25th April 1965. Evidence of High Level is limited to a signal (top right) and a puff of smoke from a freight train approaching. (P.J.Garland/R.S.Carpenter)

26. The footbridge steps (top right) and the water tank are part of High Level and were recorded on 26th September 1960. The lattice spans on the right were over the freight lines connecting the two levels. (H.C.Casserley)

VII. The 1864 Newport, Abervagenny & Hereford Railway route runs from right to left and passes over the single line viaduct into the 703yd long Quakers Yard Tunnel (just off the map) to reach the Cynon Valley. Still in use is the Merthyr to Cardiff line (top to bottom) of the TVR. It made its first connection with another standard gauge line via the curve on the right. The three viaducts shown are over the River Taff. The line on the one top left was built jointly by the GWR and RR and was opened in 1886. It ran to Merthyr via Aberfan and closed in 1951. The east-west route followed in 1964. The 1919 map is at 22ins to 1 mile.

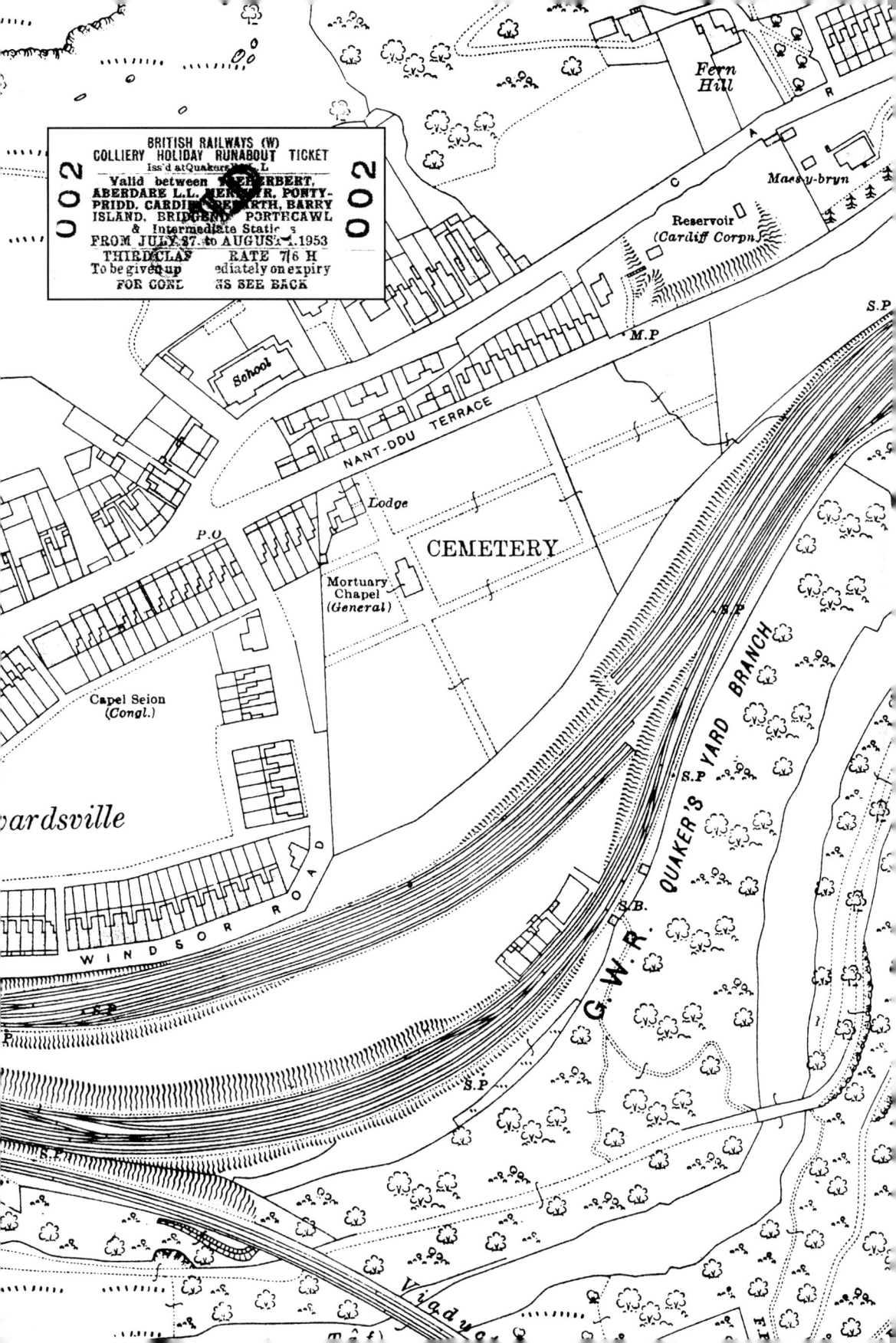

27. Seen on the same day is 0-6-2T no. 5677 with the 3.47pm Pontypridd to Merthyr, which served as the school train; the school is top right on the map. Mr. Edwards was involved in the housing development here. (H.C.Casserley)

28. An eastward panorama at about the same time features the TVR station building on the down platform and a GWR corrugated iron Pagoda shelter on the up platform. A glimpse of the exchange sidings is on the left. One telegraph pole (top left) indicates the level of the Pontypool route. (Lens of Sutton coll.)

29. Our survey is completed with a westward view from the same era, with the signal box in the distance. The Quakers were a religious group with high ideals and Yard was their term for a burial site. It was one mile to the south. There was originally nothing of note nearer to the station. (Lens of Sutton coll.)

QUAKERS YARD

30. Little modernisation took place and this is the scene in September 1998, viewed from the lower right corner of picture 28. The houses had been built on the sites of the exchange sidings and the High Level platforms. South of the station is the viaduct built by Brunel over the River Taff. It was doubled between 1862-1867 and a tunnel was eliminated at the same time. A new route was provided at an easier gradient for locomotive working allowing the rope worked incline to be abandoned in 1867. (E.Wilmshurst)

SOUTH OF MERTHYR VALE

31. In clear sunlight, Andrew Barclay no. 2340 of 1953 moves coal from Merthyr Vale Colliery (left) to Black Lion Sidings on 6th October 1971. Coal was produced here from 1875 until 1989. (T.Heavyside)

32. Black Lion Sidings box was photographed on 20th September 1981. It had earlier served between Llanelli and Cynheidre and worked here until 21st June 1992, controlling the only passing place north of Abercynon after the route had been singled in 1970. (D.K.Jones coll.)

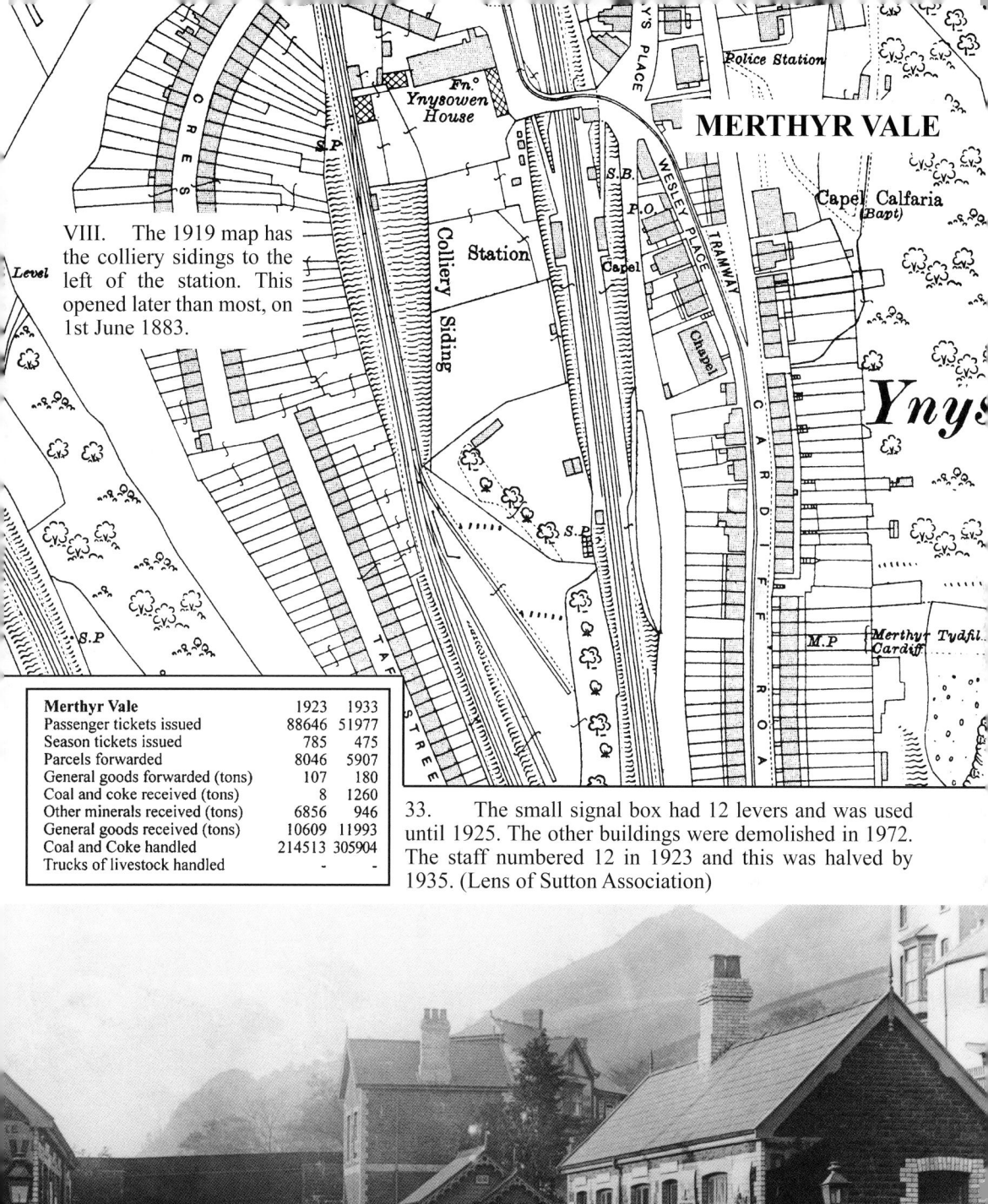

VIII. The 1919 map has the colliery sidings to the left of the station. This opened later than most, on 1st June 1883.

Merthyr Vale	1923	1933
Passenger tickets issued	88646	51977
Season tickets issued	785	475
Parcels forwarded	8046	5907
General goods forwarded (tons)	107	180
Coal and coke received (tons)	8	1260
Other minerals received (tons)	6856	946
General goods received (tons)	10609	11993
Coal and Coke handled	214513	305904
Trucks of livestock handled	-	-

33. The small signal box had 12 levers and was used until 1925. The other buildings were demolished in 1972. The staff numbered 12 in 1923 and this was halved by 1935. (Lens of Sutton Association)

34. Running through the mist on 6th March 1958 is 0-6-2T no. 5686 with the 1.00pm Barry Island to Merthyr service. (D.K.Jones coll.)

35. The 10.50 Merthyr to Barry Island on 26th March 1976 had DMU C317 at the rear. The Black Lion to Merthyr section was singled on 7th February 1971. (T.Heavyside)

36. A complete transformation had taken place after a new two-mile long passing loop was completed in 2008. Pacer no. 142072 is working from Merthyr on 13th February 2009. The complex railed inclines constitute disabled access. A 30-minute interval weekday service was possible from 17th May 2009. (V.Mitchell)

ALCOHOL POLICY

Arriva Trains Wales have prohibited the consumption of alcohol on all services and stations between Caerphilly - Rhymney, and Pontypridd - Treherbert/Merthr Tydfil/Aberdare

From RAIL TIMES (Middleton Press December 2011)

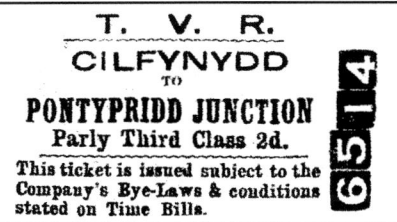

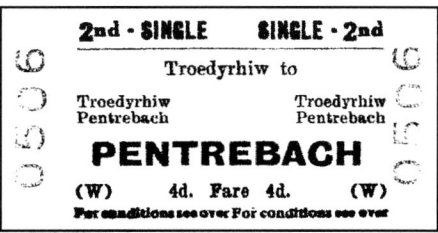

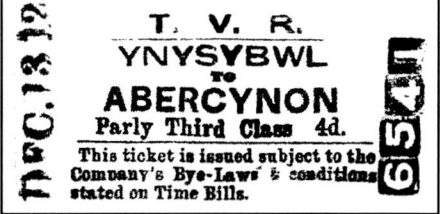

TROED-Y-RHIW

IX. The 1919 survey has a road close to its right border which had earlier had a tramway along it. It appeared to serve the rear of the properties on the east side of Chapel Street. Such lines were often used for the delivery of domestic coal and sometimes the removal of night soil. Top right is part of South Dyffryn Pit. The signal box (near the goods shed) had 12 levers and lasted until 1925.

37. The station appears to have been opened with the line, or soon after. Its name included two hyphens from 12th May 1980 and it is seen in about 1960. Its small goods yard closed on 7th October 1963. There were 15 employees in 1923, but only 9 by 1931. (Lens of Sutton Association)

38. The western platform remained in use after the 1971 singling and is seen in July 1980. Forty years later, it was still listed as taking seven coaches. (D.K.Jones coll.)

Troedyrhiw	1923	1933
Passenger tickets issued	101439	86517
Season tickets issued	664	623
Parcels forwarded	11773	10576
General goods forwarded (tons)	134	107
Coal and coke received (tons)	94	562
Other minerals received (tons)	1925	71
General goods received (tons)	2100	1519
Coal and Coke handled	1852	179
Trucks of livestock handled	-	-

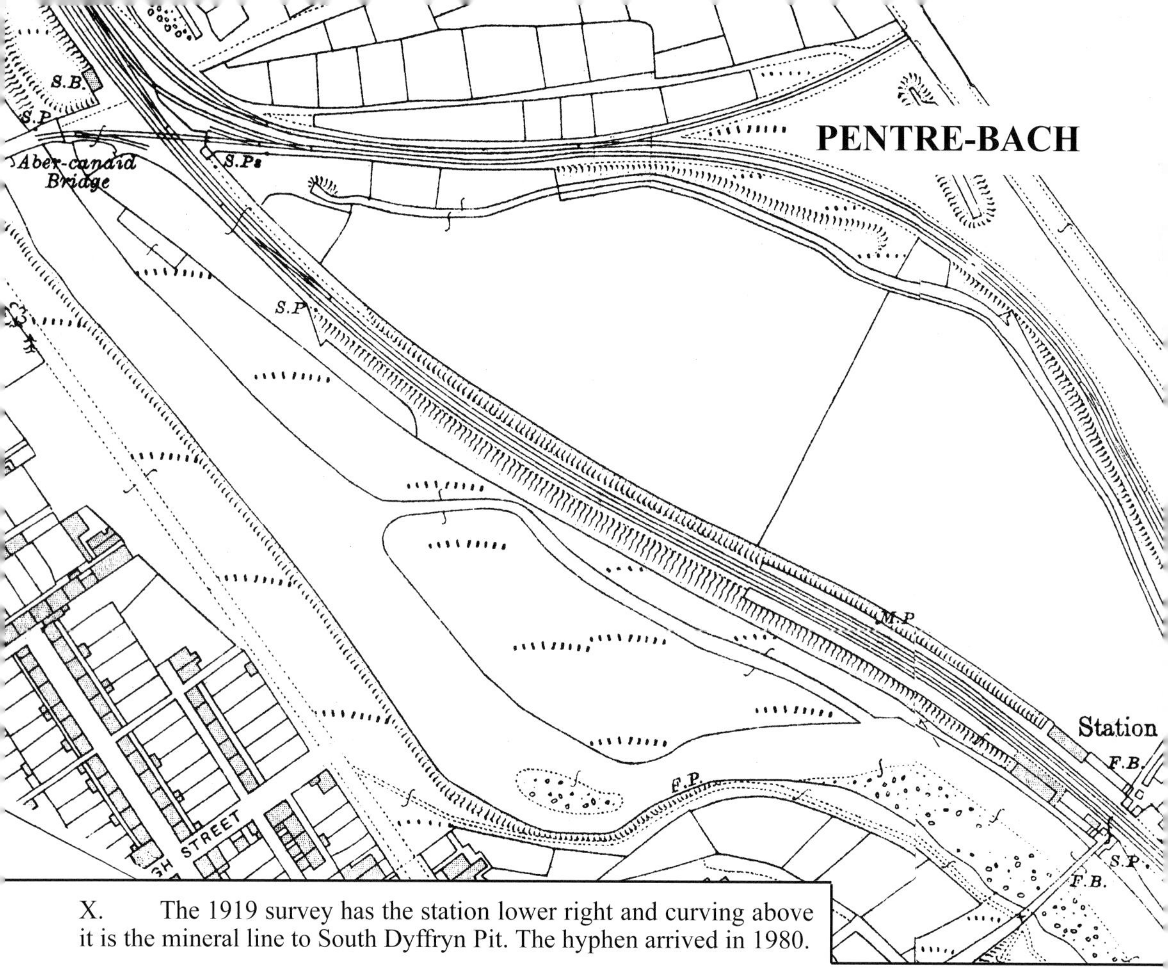

PENTRE-BACH

X. The 1919 survey has the station lower right and curving above it is the mineral line to South Dyffryn Pit. The hyphen arrived in 1980.

39. The station opened on 1st August 1886 and was linked to its community by this footbridge. There was no goods traffic, but the map shows two colliery lines ending at roads, probably for local supplies. (Lens of Sutton Association)

40. A 1958 view includes part of the running-in board for PENTREBACH FOR ABERCANAID, which BR replaced before the next photograph. There were eight men here in 1923, but this was down to six by 1932. (Stations UK)

41. From the 1960s, this southward view features the massive accommodation for gentlemen, with very generous ventilation. The left platform remained in use in 2011, but all the buildings shown had long gone. (Lens of Sutton coll.)

SOUTH OF MERTHYR

42. This northward panorama from 4th May 1955 is at Brandy Bridge Junction, which is lower right on the next map. Featured is 5700 class 0-6-0PT no. 7766 and the original terminus was just beyond the viaduct in the background. The box had 42 levers and was in use until 21st November 1967. (M.Hale)

Extract from Bradshaws Guide of 1866. (Reprinted by Middleton Press in 2011)

MERTHYR.

POPULATION 83,875.
A telegraph station.
HOTELS.—Castle Bush.
MARKET DAYS.—Wednesday and Saturday.
BANKERS. — Wilkins and Co.; Branch of West of England and South Wales District Banking Company.

MERTHYR TYDVIL is a parliamentary borough, and great mining town, in South Wales, 21 miles from Cardiff, with which there is railway communication by a branch out of the South Wales line. It stands up the Taff, among the rugged and barren-looking hills in the north-east corner of Glamorganshire, the richest county in Wales for mineral wealth. About a century ago the first iron works were established here, since which the extension has been amazingly rapid. Blast furnaces, forges, and rolling mills are scattered on all sides. Each iron furnace is about 55 feet high, containing 5,000 cubic feet; and capable of smelting 100 tons of pig-iron weekly, and as there are upwards of 50, the annual quantity of metal may be tolerably estimated; but great as that supply may seem, it is scarcely equal to the demand created for it by railways. The largest works are those belonging to Lady Guest and Messrs. Crawshay, where 3,000 to 5,000 hands are employed. At Guest's Dowlais works there are 18 or 20 blast furnaces, besides many furnaces for puddling, balling, and refining; and 1,000 tons of coal a day are consumed.

Visitors should see the furnaces by night, when the red glare of the flames produces an uncommonly striking effect. Indeed, the town is best visited at that time, for by day it will be found dirty, and irregularly built, without order or management, decent roads or footpaths, no supply of water, and no public building of the least note, except Barracks, and a vast *Poor-House*, lately finished, in the shape of a cross, on heaps of the rubbish accumulated from the pits and works. Cholera and fever are, of course, at home here, in scenes which would shock even the most "eminent defender of the filth," and which imperatively demand that their Lady owner should become one of "the Nightingale sisterhood" for a brief space of time. Out of 695 couples married in 1845, 1,016 persons signed with marks, one great secret of which social drawback is the unexampled rapidity with which the town has sprung up; but we do hope that proper measures will be taken henceforth by those who draw enormous wealth from working these works, to improve the condition of the people. Coal and iron are found together in this part of Wales, the coal being worked mostly by levels, in beds 2 to 3 feet thick.

43. This photograph features Plymouth Street Goods Depot from the south on 3rd May 1964. This had been the site of the TVR terminus until 1st August 1877, when trains were diverted to High Street station. (P.J.Garland/R.S.Carpenter)

44. The one imposing north elevation had been adorned by pipework for four different functions by the time it was recorded in 1958. Traffic ceased on 27th November 1967. (Stations UK)

XI. The 1922 edition at 6in to 1 mile has our route lower right, aptly, close to the River Taff. The original terminus is shaded (near The Court) and the High Street one is black. Trains from the south use the spur up on to the viaduct. High Street was used by the Vale of Neath Railway (from 2nd November 1853), the London & North Western Railway (from 1st June 1868), the Brecon & Merthyr Railway (from 1st August 1868) and the TVR plus the GWR (from 1st August 1877). The Rhymney Railway followed on 1st April 1886.

45. A train is running north on the viaduct on 3rd May 1964 and our route is joining from the right. On the far left is the long roof of the engine shed. (P.J.Garland/R.S.Carpenter)

46. A northward view of the Merthyr engine shed and pits in 1938 shows the 1932 roof extension. The signal box to the left was built in 1934 and its 77-lever frame was in use until 7th February 1971. (D.K.Jones coll.)

47. The adjacent coal stage is under the roof and the 55ft turntable is on the left. The shed was in use from 1877 until November 1964. It had 20 engines (0-6-0PTs or 0-6-2Ts) in 1947 and was coded 88D by BR. (Colour-Rail.com)

MERTHYR

48. The five platforms were photographed in the mid-1920s. On the right is the large granary. The platforms were often used to capacity in the Summer for excursions to the coast. (D.K.Jones coll.)

49. The same view in September 1951 reveals that the centre platform was of timber construction. This had arrived following the removal of the broad gauge VofNR tracks. The goods shed is on the right. (Lens of Sutton Association)

50. The old buildings were swept away in the early 1970s and one with a flat roof and white barge boards appeared, along with a modern canopy. They are seen on 13th September 1973 as no. C303 waits to leave for Barry Island. (D.H.Mitchell)

51. A replica of Richard Trevithick's historic locomotive of 1804 was built by the Welsh Industrial and Maritime Museum and was on display in the station on 25th July 1981. It ran on the 1802 Penydaren Tramway, evidence of which can be found on some of the maps between here and Abercynon. The line was of 4ft 4ins gauge and the cast iron rails were 3ft long. (P.Jones)

52. The station seen in pictures 50 and 51 was dismantled in 1996-97 to allow for a major supermarket development. The replacement was further south and is seen on 13th February 2009. (V.Mitchell)

53. The end of the line and the oily patches of the termination point were recorded on 7th August 2011. Brunel's styling is evident, as is the enthusiastic detail of the Service Frequency Enhancement notice. (D.K.Jones)

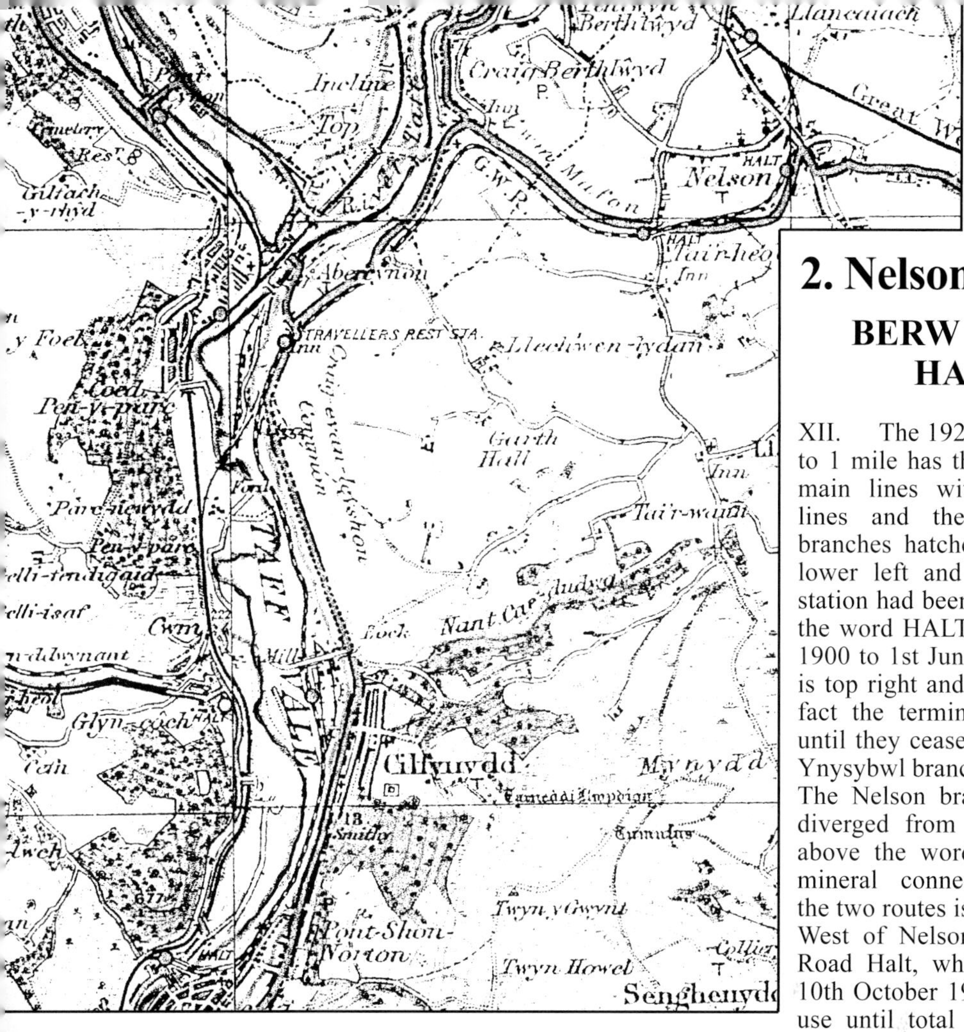

2. Nelson Branch
BERW ROAD HALT

XII. The 1922 map at 1½ins to 1 mile has the double track main lines with solid black lines and the single track branches hatched. The halt is lower left and Coedpenmaen station had been to the right of the word HALT from 1st June 1900 to 1st June 1915. Nelson is top right and its halt was in fact the terminus of services until they ceased in 1932. The Ynysybwl branch is on the left. The Nelson branch originally diverged from the main line above the word TAFF and a mineral connection between the two routes is shown feintly. West of Nelson is Llanfabon Road Halt, which opened on 10th October 1904 and was in use until total closure of the route on 12th September 1932.

54. The branch and the halt are on the right of this view from a northbound train on 5th June 1960. The main lines were flanked by freight lines from 1908. The first halt was open from 17th October 1904 to 1st July 1906, but was located on the main line to Merthyr. The one seen here on the Pont Shon Norton Branch was open from July 1908 until 12th September 1932. The first platform was just a framework structure. The large building was a sweet factory for many years. HALT was added to the name on 2nd October 1922. (M.Dart/Transport Treasury)

XIII. The 1919 edition has the halt near the right border. To the right of the Old Quarry is Pont Shon Norton signal box, which has been seen in picture no. 10. The gated siding (top) was for Graig-yr-Hesg Quarry.

CILFYNYDD

← XIV. The 1915 survey at 20ins to 1 mile has the station on the left, with a very long footbridge leading to it from a passing loop on the electric tramway to Pontypridd (1905-30).

55. The Cilfynydd Loop is seen under construction in about 1898. Albion Colliery was 1900ft deep and is in the background. The station would be built close to it and the new line would link Cilfynydd with Travellers Rest. (A.Dudman coll.)

56. The TVR station had generous weather protection, in a similar style to the GWR of the period. It was open to passengers from 1st June 1900 until 12th September 1932 and for freight until the end of 1949. (GWR)

57. The platform was close to Albion Colliery and remained to be photographed on 29th July 1960. The pit had been started in 1884 and coal production began in 1887. It ended in September 1966. All traffic ceased north of here in 1932. (M.Hale)

TRAVELLERS REST HALT

58. Dowlais Cardiff Colliery is seen from the east on a postcard from about 1910 and the small station building is lower left, along with TVR's complex telegraph wiring. The halt opened on 18th March 1902 and closed with the line. It had the suffix "Abercynon Upper" until 1st July 1924. (A.Dudman coll.)

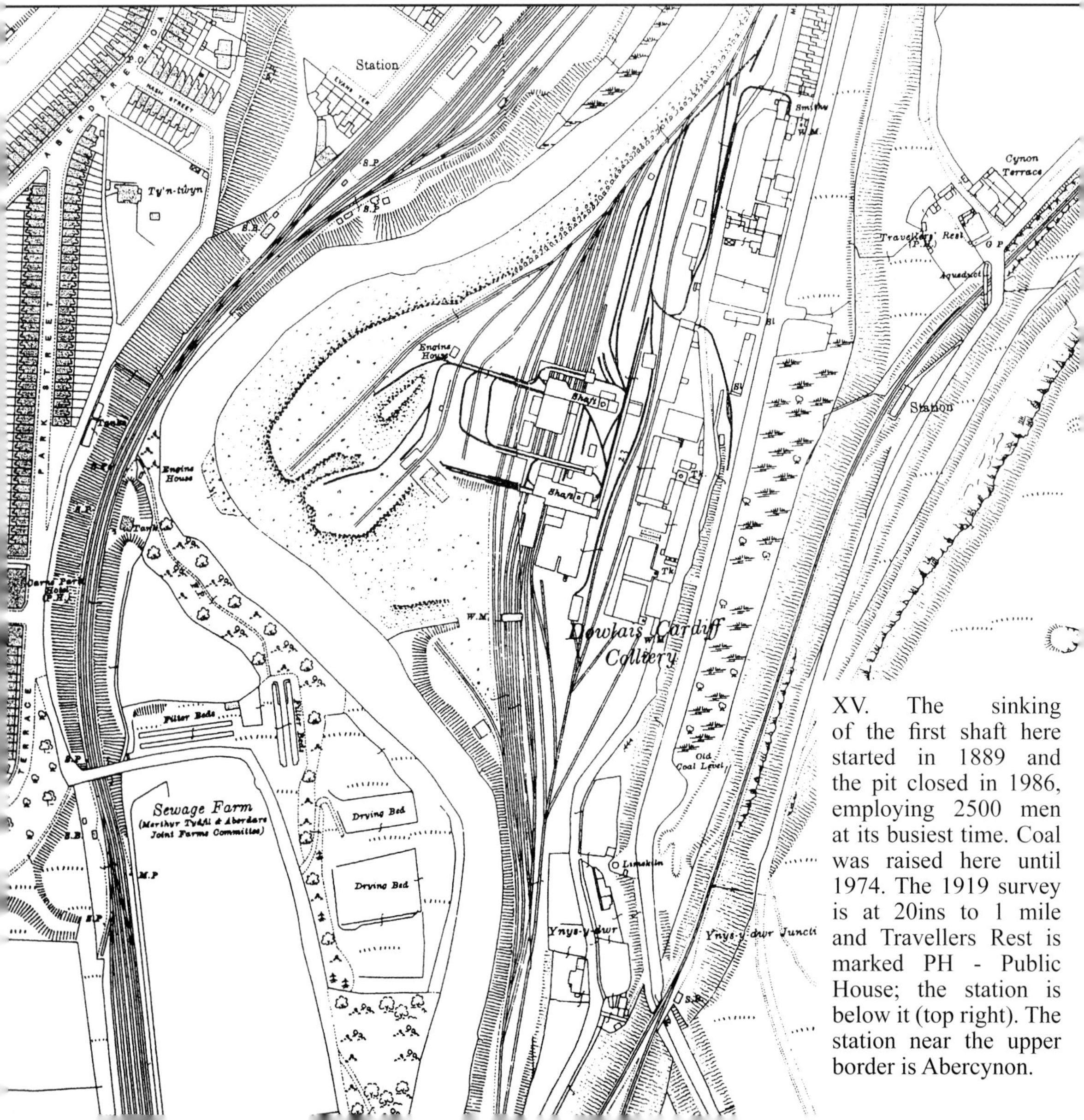

XV. The sinking of the first shaft here started in 1889 and the pit closed in 1986, employing 2500 men at its busiest time. Coal was raised here until 1974. The 1919 survey is at 20ins to 1 mile and Travellers Rest is marked PH - Public House; the station is below it (top right). The station near the upper border is Abercynon.

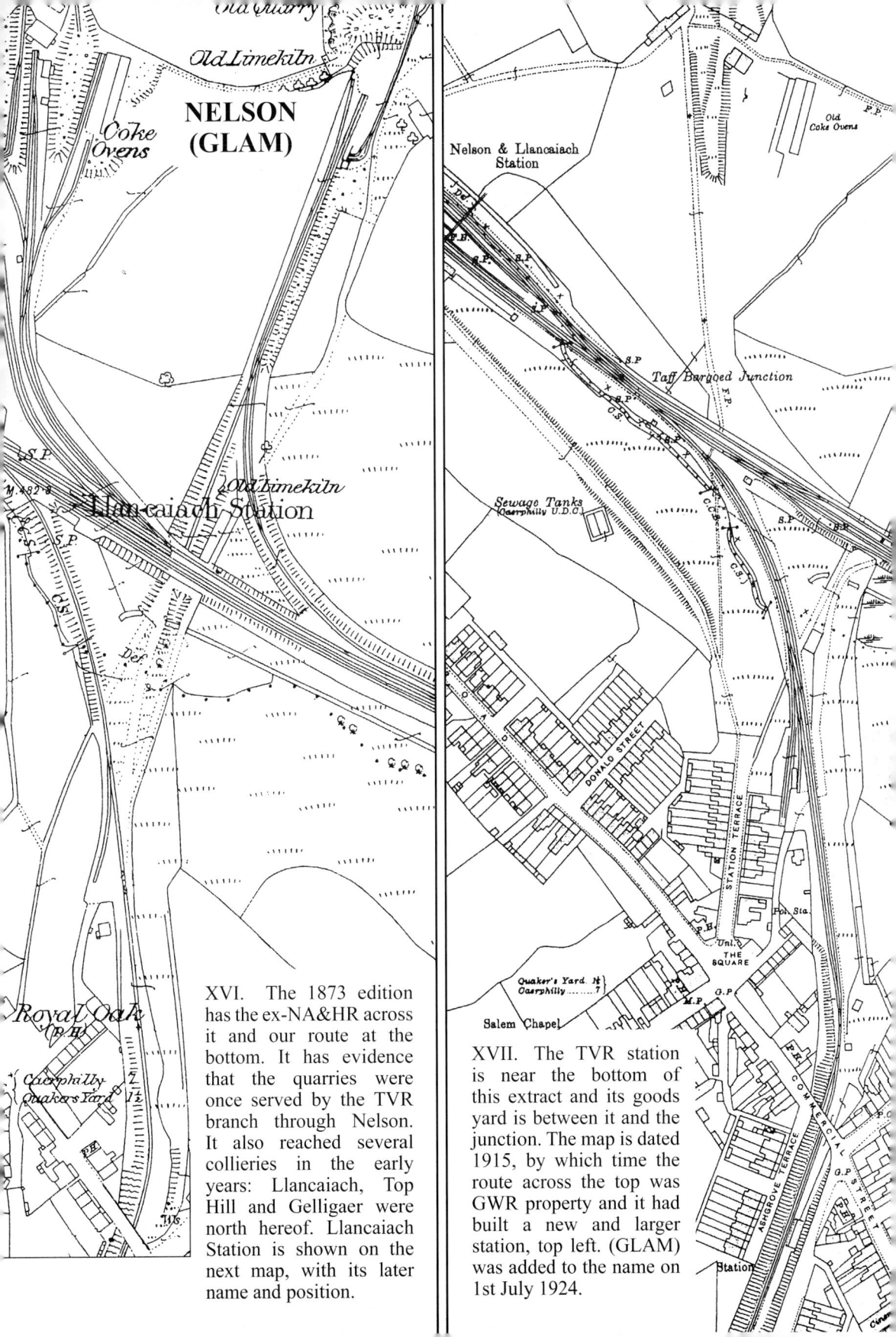

XVI. The 1873 edition has the ex-NA&HR across it and our route at the bottom. It has evidence that the quarries were once served by the TVR branch through Nelson. It also reached several collieries in the early years: Llancaiach, Top Hill and Gelligaer were north hereof. Llancaiach Station is shown on the next map, with its later name and position.

XVII. The TVR station is near the bottom of this extract and its goods yard is between it and the junction. The map is dated 1915, by which time the route across the top was GWR property and it had built a new and larger station, top left. (GLAM) was added to the name on 1st July 1924.

59. Here was another station named after a local public house. It seems that the labourers who arrived in vast numbers from outside Wales could not cope with the complexities of Ffos-y-Gerddinen. There had been a goods yard here until 5th August 1912, but its traffic was transferred thereafter to the new station at Nelson & Llancaiach. There was a run-round loop north of the bridge. (Lens of Sutton Association)

60. A southward view in about 1936 shows the limit of the line from Llancaiach, which was retained for wagon storage after the remainder of the line was closed and lifted in 1932. The junction with the NA&HR at Nelson & Llancaiach can be seen in pictures 76-87 in our *Pontypool to Mountain Ash* album. However, passenger trains did not run north of the station seen here. There was the luxury of a signal box from 1900 to 1907. The station was used by the Home Guard during World War II. The staff had numbered four in 1923, but there were only two from 1929. (Stations UK)

3. Ynysybwl Branch
CLYDACH COURT HALT

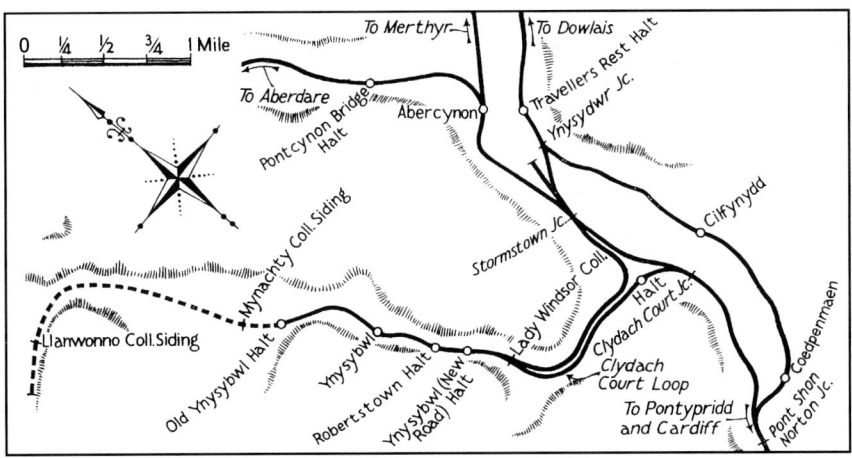

XVIII. The diagram shows the routes in 1952, although freight trains had not been able to reach Dowlais via Nelson since 1932; steel making had ceased there in 1930. Stormstown Junction had been the access point to both branches in the 19th century. The Clydach Court Loop, west from Clydach Court Junction, came into use in 1900. The passenger service over it began on 17th October 1904, but the halt did not open until July 1917. The dashes indicate the former route to collieries. (Railway Magazine)

61. Passenger service ceased on the branch on 28th July 1952 and this photograph was taken soon after. It is a typical TVR halt, where passengers were held in a compound at the back of it until the train had stopped. The guard would then emerge and unlock the gate to allow them onto the platform. (R.C.Riley/Transport Treasury)

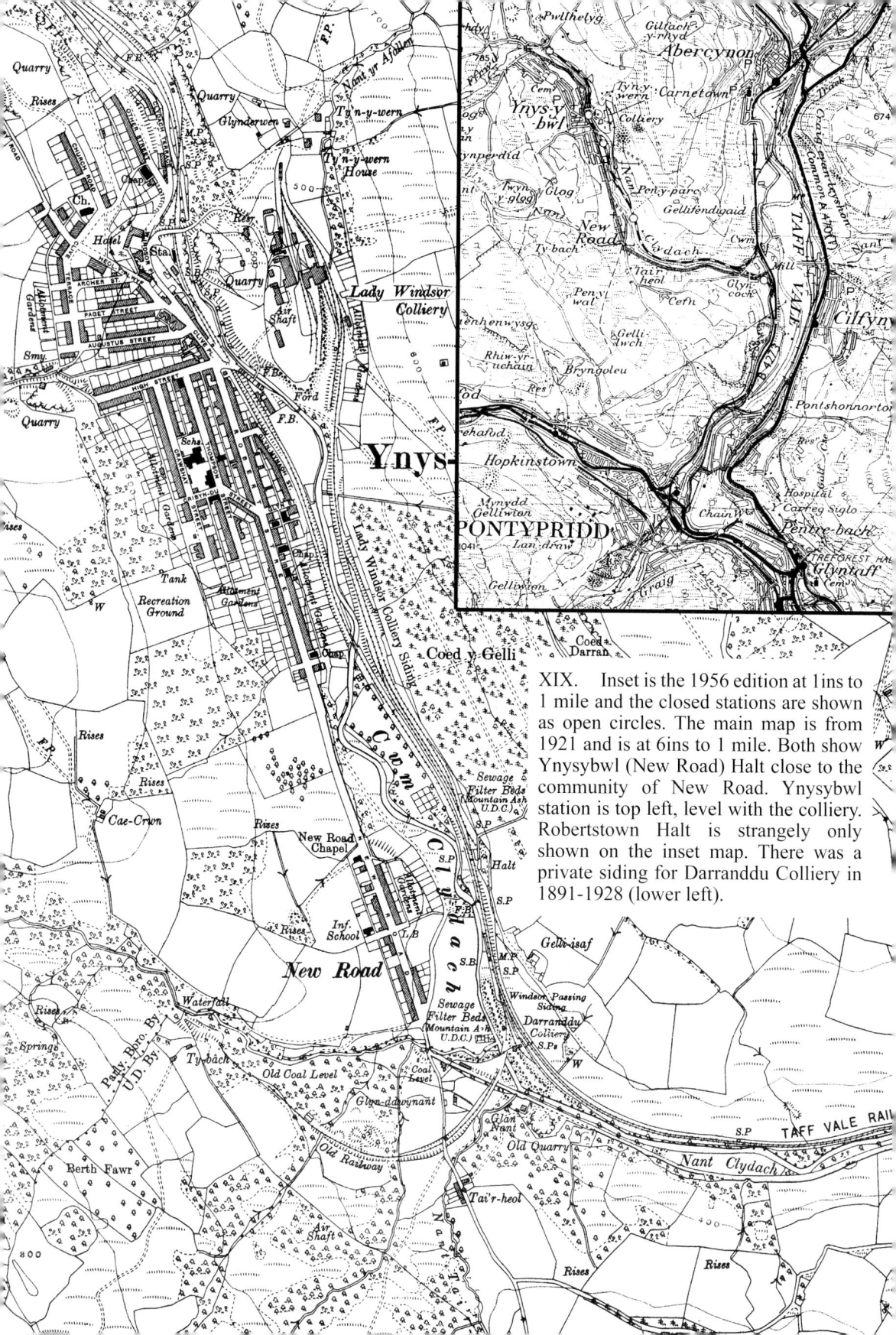

XIX. Inset is the 1956 edition at 1ins to 1 mile and the closed stations are shown as open circles. The main map is from 1921 and is at 6ins to 1 mile. Both show Ynysybwl (New Road) Halt close to the community of New Road. Ynysybwl station is top left, level with the colliery. Robertstown Halt is strangely only shown on the inset map. There was a private siding for Darranddu Colliery in 1891-1928 (lower left).

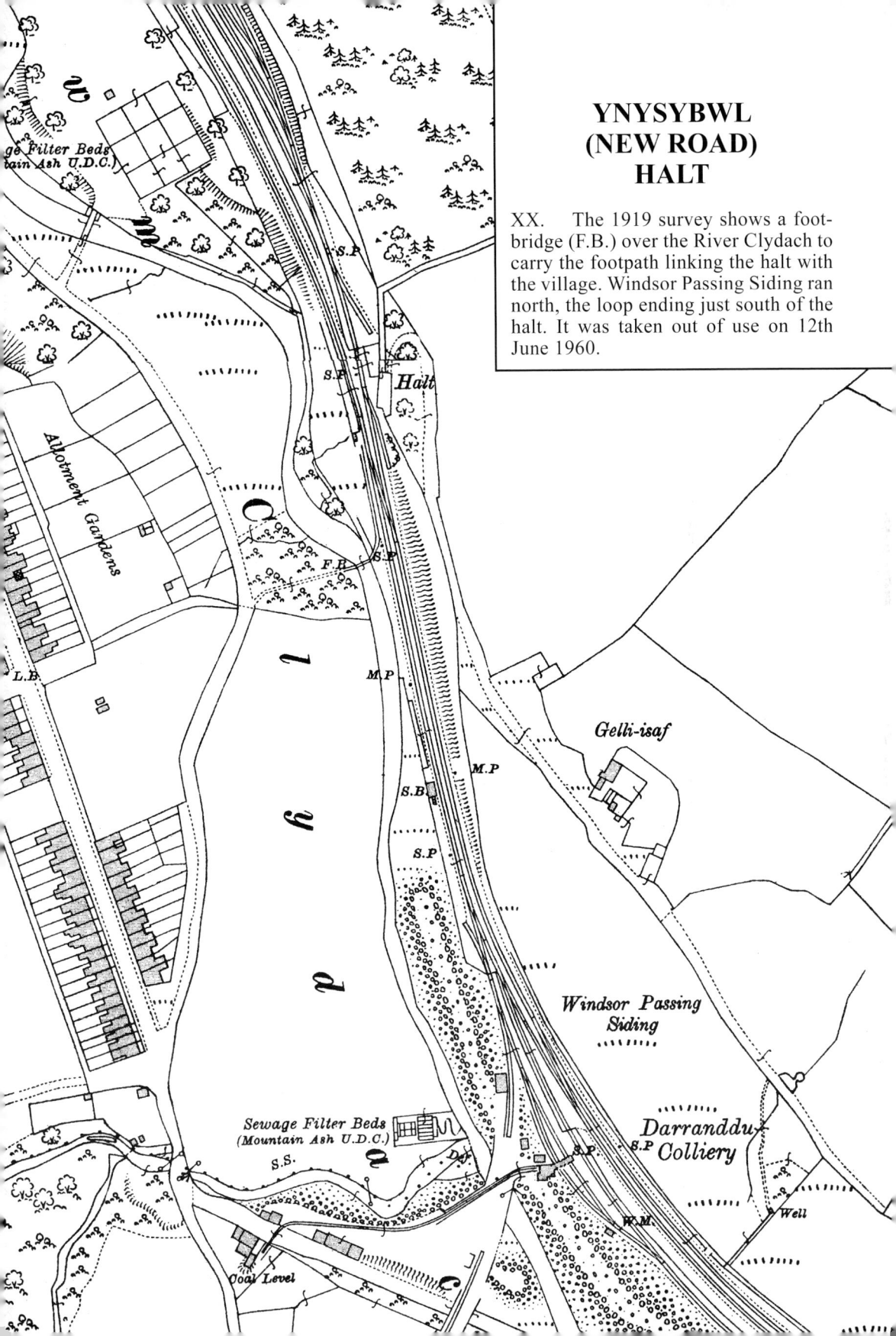

YNYSYBWL (NEW ROAD) HALT

XX. The 1919 survey shows a footbridge (F.B.) over the River Clydach to carry the footpath linking the halt with the village. Windsor Passing Siding ran north, the loop ending just south of the halt. It was taken out of use on 12th June 1960.

62. Little remained of the halt when visited in 1959. Lady Windsor Colliery sidings begin in the background. (M.Hale)

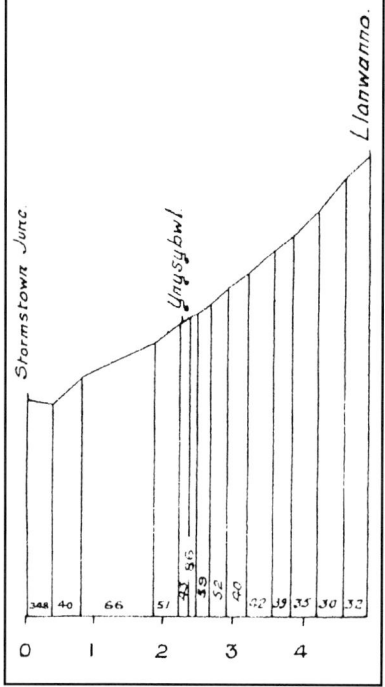

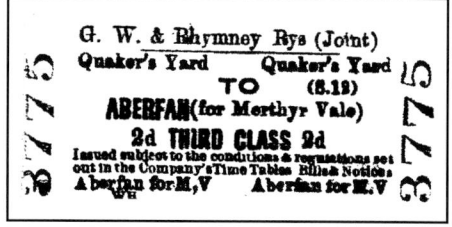

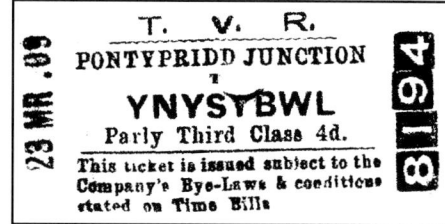

ROBERTSTOWN HALT

63. This view across the valley is from about 1904, prior to the provision of a shelter. The TVR used steam railmotors on most of their branches, from about that time until GWR takeover. (A.Dudman coll.)

64. As elsewhere, a fenced pen with a locked gate was provided, but unusually a shelter was erected over it, on an unknown date. Initially Robertstown Platform, it became Robertstown Halt on 2nd October 1922 and was even electrically lit. (British Railways)

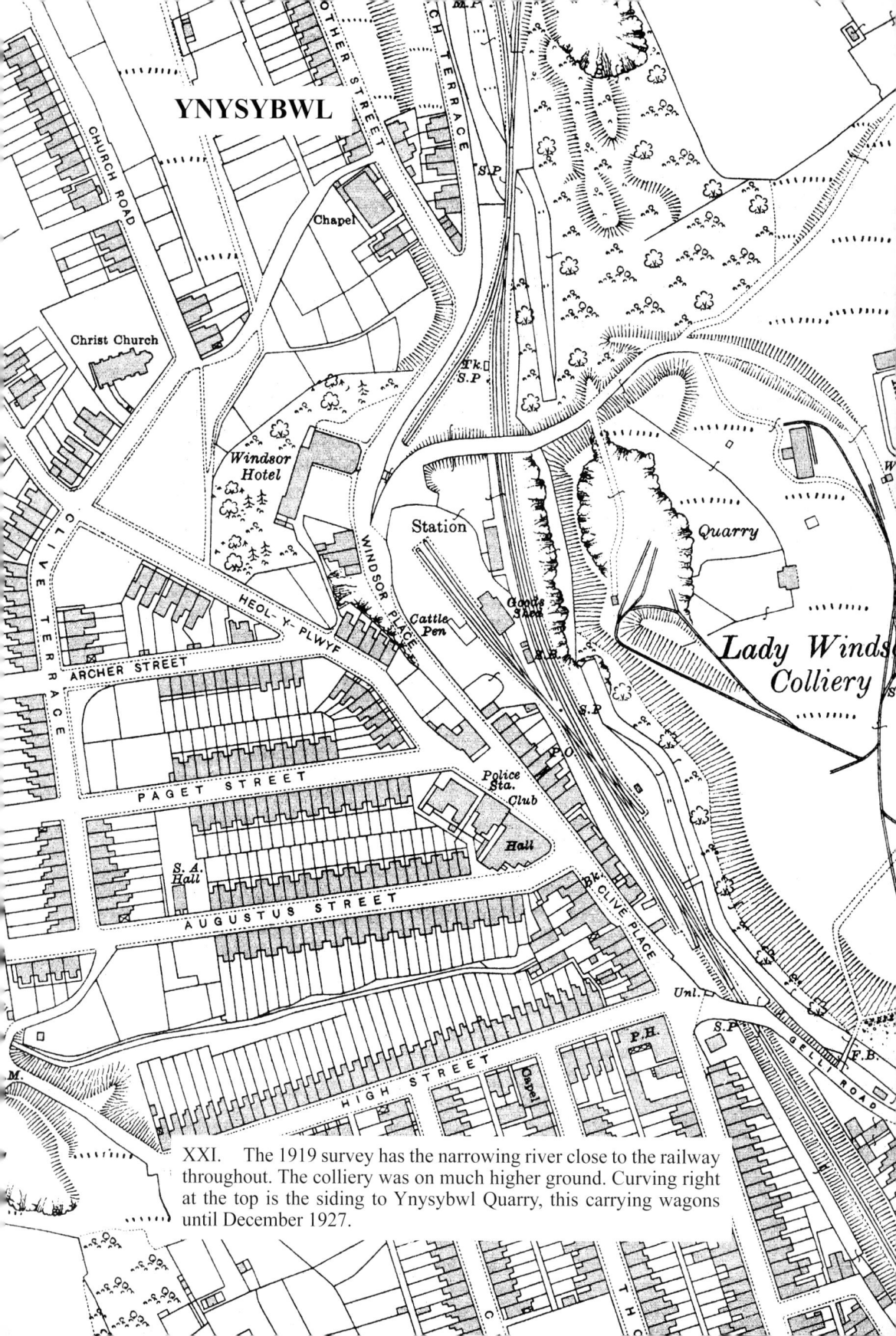

XXI. The 1919 survey has the narrowing river close to the railway throughout. The colliery was on much higher ground. Curving right at the top is the siding to Ynysybwl Quarry, this carrying wagons until December 1927.

65. The station is on the left and the goods shed is centre as we look south through the dust and smoke. The staff numbered 12 in 1923 and 8 ten years later. (Lens of Sutton Association)

66. Ynysybwl station was visited by a railtour on 11th July 1959. The signal box had 25 levers and was the only one on the branch, north of Windsor Passing Sidings Box. The station building later became a surgery. (Stations UK)

Ynysybwl	1923	1933
Passenger tickets issued	10290	4356
Season tickets issued	56899	21956
Parcels forwarded	9308	3564
General goods forwarded (tons)	358	472
Coal and coke received (tons)	68	7
Other minerals received (tons)	1985	999
General goods received (tons)	14551	9392
Coal and Coke handled	338691	256368
Trucks of livestock handled	140	76

67. This northward view is from the bridge at the north end of the station on the same day. Next up the valley had been Ynysybwl Quarry (1913-27), Mynachdy Colliery (1903-33), then Black Grove (1884-1903) and finally Llanwonno (1901-04). The goods yard lasted until 2nd November 1959. (D.K.Jones coll.)

68. This glimpse into Lady Windsor Colliery was on 19th May 1976 and includes Hunslet 0-6-0ST no. 3829 of 1950. Two tunnels, each almost one mile long, linked it to Abercynon Colliery in 1974 and high speed belts brought coal from it to here, where it was raised in modern spiral shafts. Both pits were closed in 1986 and the last coal train left here on 20th May 1988. (D.K.Jones coll.)

OLD YNYSYBWL HALT

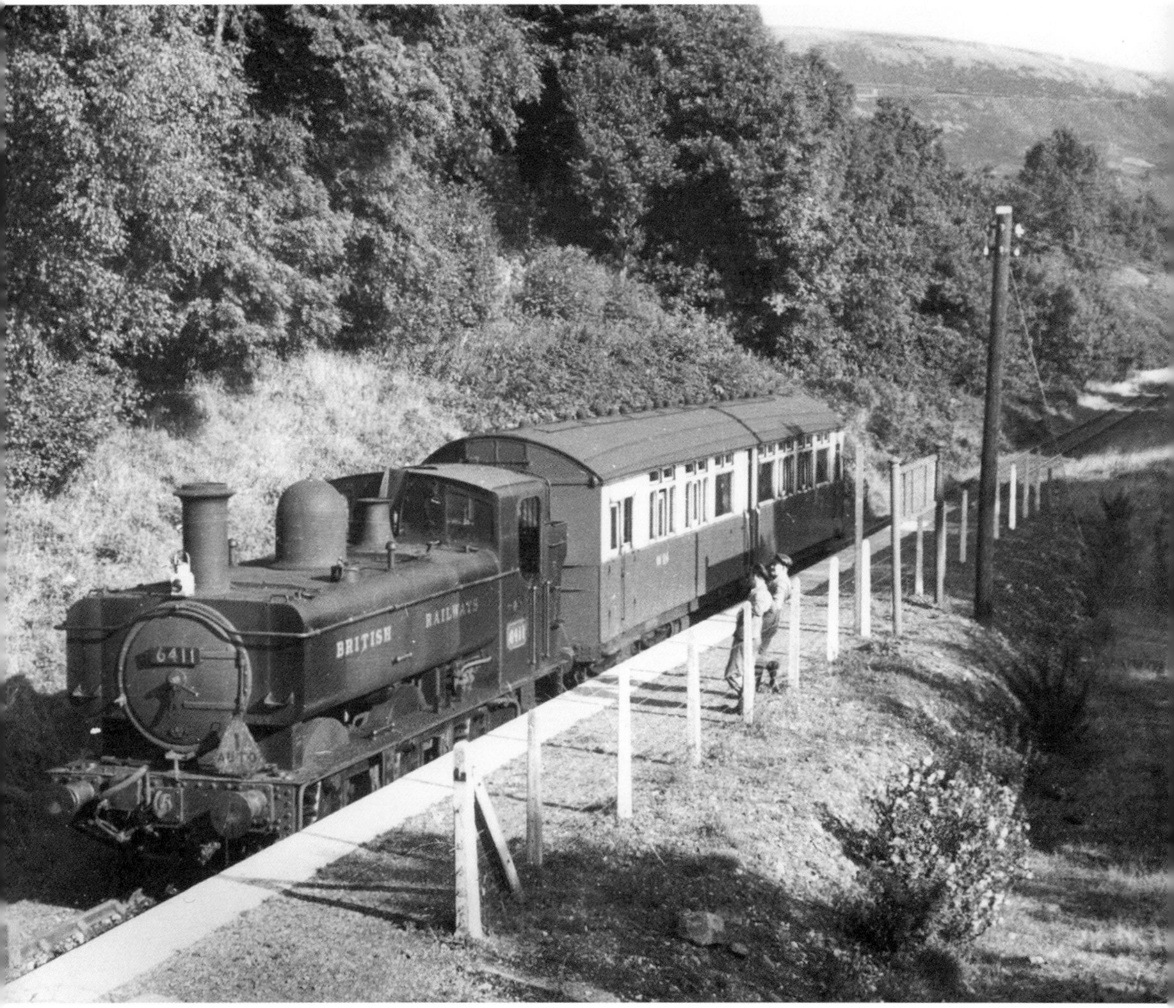

69. This is the final station on the branch and is seen on 11th September 1951 with the 4.23pm from Pontypridd and no. 6411 with autotrailer no. 114. Here also, the term PLATFORM was used until 1922. This was a pleasant rural destination for Sunday School outings. The new platform appeared in 1949 and the buffer stop arrived in 1950. (H.C.Casserley)

1004
BRITISH RLYS (W) BRITISH RLYS (W)
Ynysybwl Ynysybwl
TO
OLD YNYSYBWL HALT
THIRD CLASS
3d Z Fare 3d Z
Old Ynysybwl Old Ynysybwl
FOR CONDITIONS FOR CONDITIONS
SEE BACK SEE BACK E.B
1004

T. V. R.
ABERAMAN
TO
ABERDARE
First Class 4d.
This ticket is issued subject to the Company's Bye Laws and conditions stated on Time Bills
239

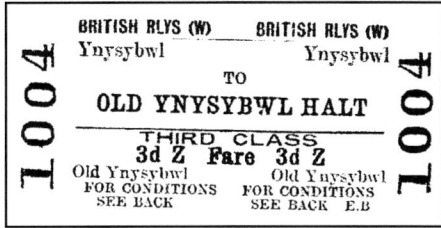

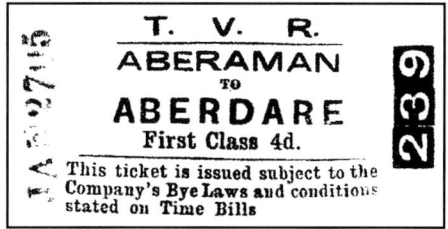

4. Quakers Yard to Merthyr
QUAKERS YARD HIGH LEVEL

70. Although the TVR opened in 1841, there was no station here until 5th January 1858, when the NA&HR opened its Taff Vale branch from Pontypool to the High Level platforms. This is the westbound platform in the Edwardian era. (A.Dudman coll.)

Other views of this station can be seen in pictures 25 to 32 herein and in nos 95 to 108 in our *Pontypool to Mountain Ash* album.

71. An eastward view in 1964 has the fence of the path to Edwardsville top left. The village of Quakers Yard was almost one mile to the south. The suffixes were added on 1st July 1924 and were not needed after 15th June 1964, when the east-west service ceased. (Stations UK)

WEST OF QUAKERS YARD

72. The line to Merthyr was double throughout and it is seen curving right. The junction is on the left page of map VII, near picture 25. The Vale of Neath line is on the left in this 1956 view. (P.J.Garland/R.S.Carpenter)

73. The first viaduct on our route north was 220yds long and had eight arches. It was deemed unsafe as much ballast had vanished one night in February 1951. It was photographed in 1956, with part of Edwardsville in the background. Demolition followed in 1969, along with the one on the former NA&HR line. Both had been given timber strengthening, due to mining subsidence, from about 1918. (P.J.Garland/R.S.Carpenter)

74. A 1958 eastward panorama features a train bound for Merthyr on the ex-TVR route. The rear coaches are under the east end of the viaduct. (S.Rickard/J&J coll.)

XXII. Pont y Gwaith is the bridge at the top and it is over the River Taff. A halt was named after it, but only the steps to the up platform and the path to the down one show on this 1919 extract. It was in use from 5th June 1905 until 1st October 1914.

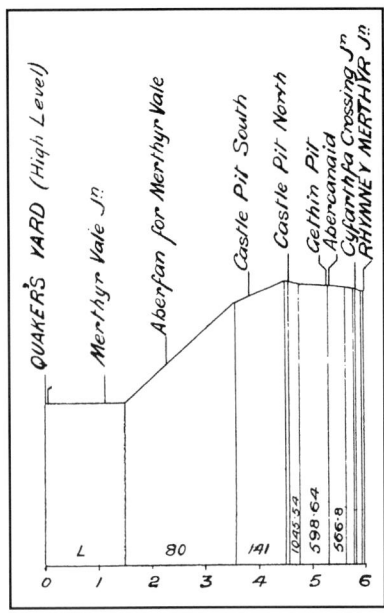

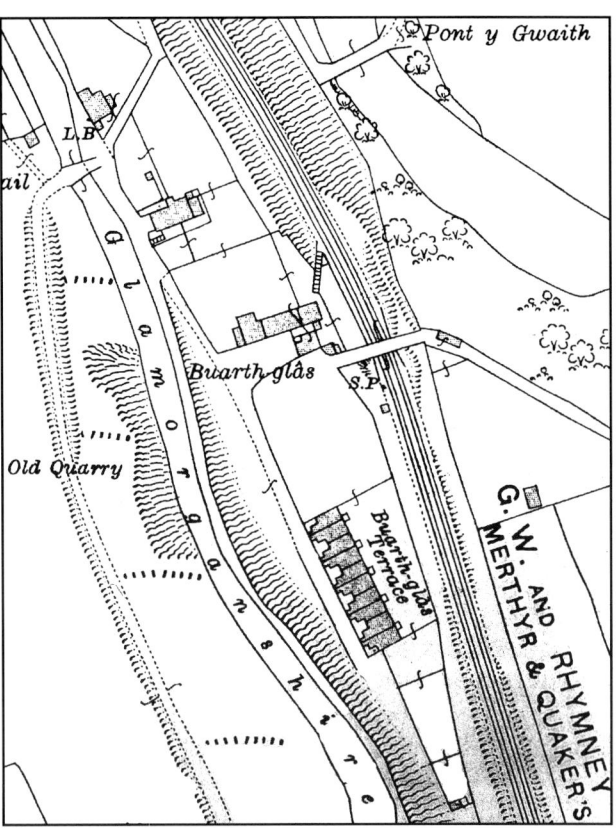

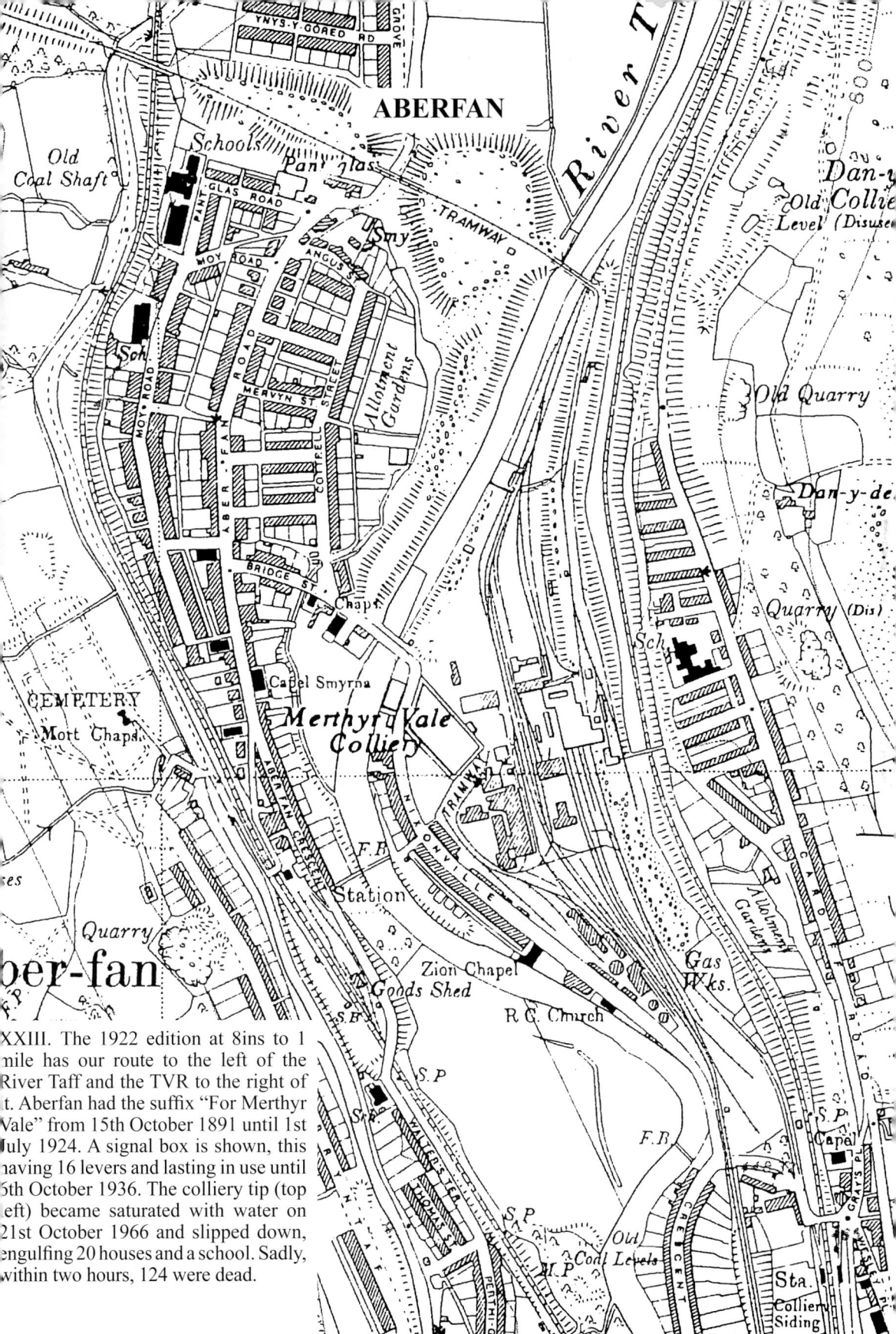

XXIII. The 1922 edition at 8ins to 1 mile has our route to the left of the River Taff and the TVR to the right of it. Aberfan had the suffix "For Merthyr Vale" from 15th October 1891 until 1st July 1924. A signal box is shown, this having 16 levers and lasting in use until 5th October 1936. The colliery tip (top left) became saturated with water on 21st October 1966 and slipped down, engulfing 20 houses and a school. Sadly, within two hours, 124 were dead.

75. The substantial building was photographed from the west in 1934. The bridge in the background is shown on the map as carrying a colliery tramway over the River Taff. (R.M.Casserley coll.)

76. Garages are on the site of the goods yard, which was used until 1st November 1954, as was the route north to Cynfarthfa Crossing. This southward view is from 1964. (Stations UK)

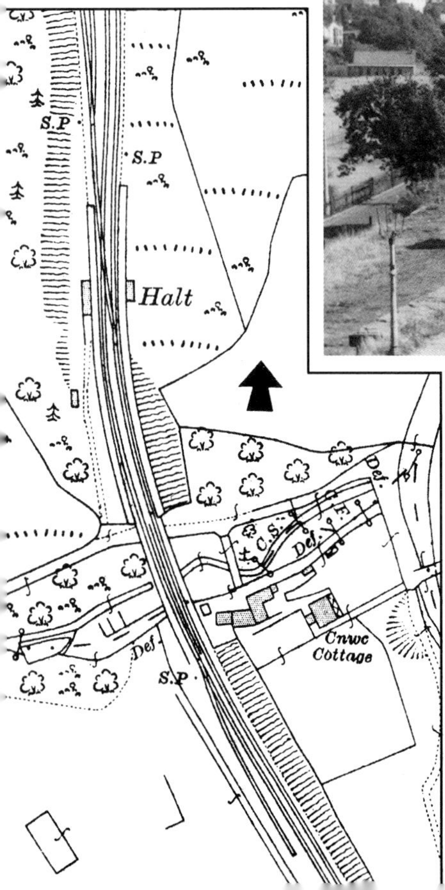

XXIV. North of the station was Troedyrhiw Halt, which was open from 18th February 1907 until line closure. It is shown on the 1922 edition, but eluded our photographers.

ABERCANAID

XXV. The 1919 edition has part of the village top right. The suffix "& Pentrebach" was in use from 9th September 1913 until 1st July 1924.

77. Passing the goods shed in April 1955 is 0-6-0PT no. 6416 with an inspection saloon. The goods yard closed on 9th May 1960. The signal box (left) had 41 levers and the track north of it was double until September 1936. The upper two sidings on the right served Gethin Pit No. 2. (N.Leek)

NORTH OF ABERCANAID

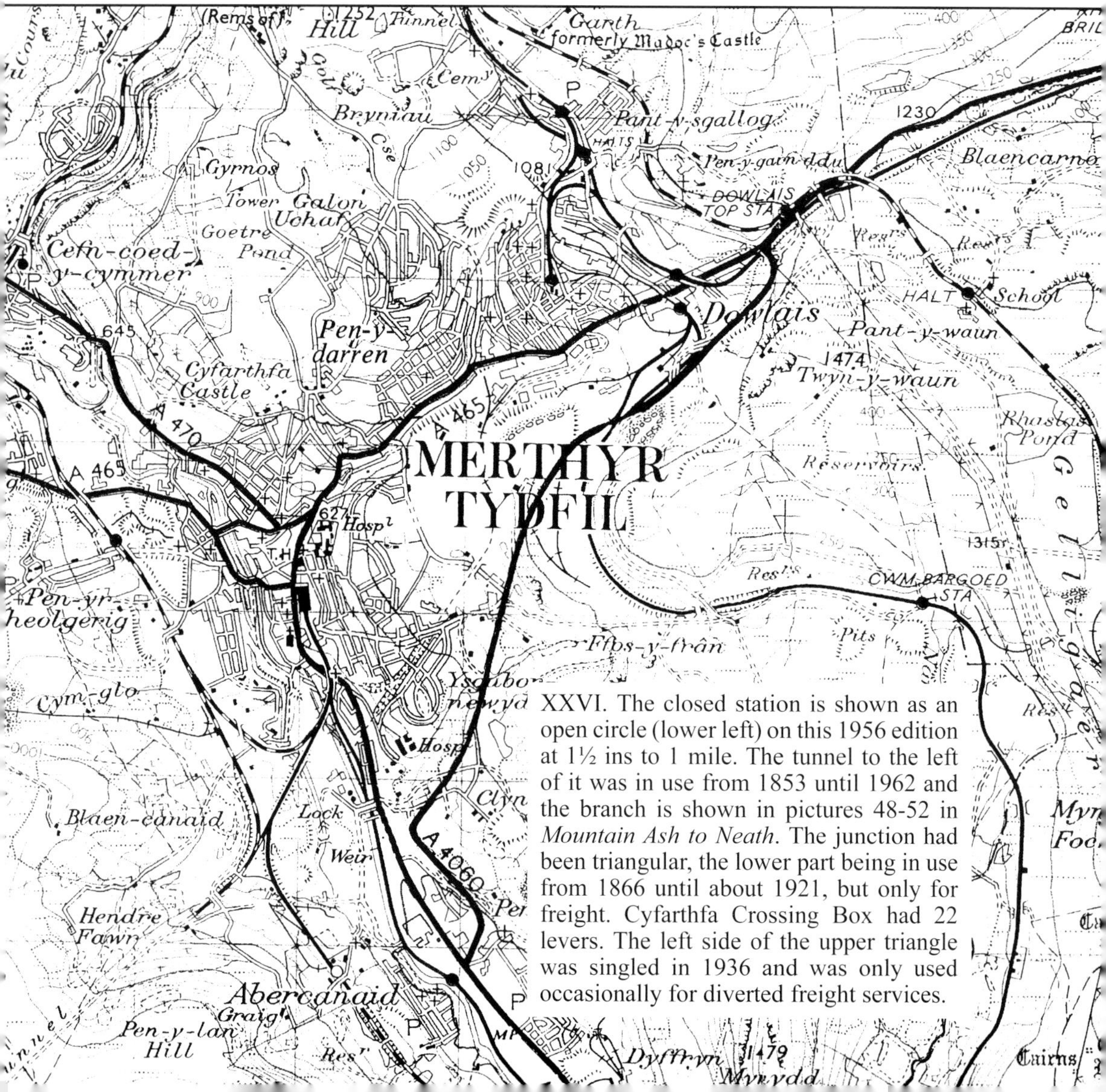

XXVI. The closed station is shown as an open circle (lower left) on this 1956 edition at 1½ ins to 1 mile. The tunnel to the left of it was in use from 1853 until 1962 and the branch is shown in pictures 48-52 in *Mountain Ash to Neath*. The junction had been triangular, the lower part being in use from 1866 until about 1921, but only for freight. Cyfarthfa Crossing Box had 22 levers. The left side of the upper triangle was singled in 1936 and was only used occasionally for diverted freight services.

5. Dare & Aman Branch

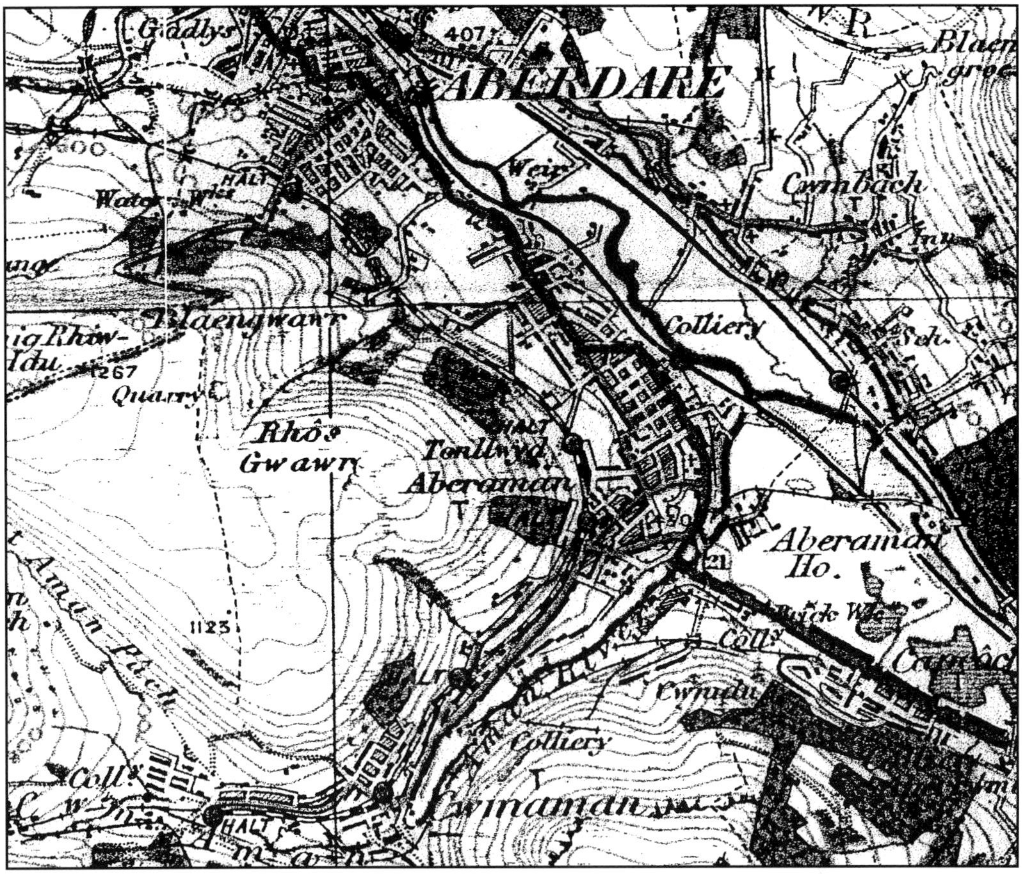

XXVII. Before our final journey, along the branch to Aberdare, we will look at a nearby line, which was very unusual in that it had no passenger interchange facilities with its parent company, the GWR. It is shown as a rough semi-circle, with a hatched line, while the two double tracks to Aberdare have solid lines. The 1922 map is at 2ins to 1 mile. The route starts top left at Black Lion Crossing Halt and passes through four halts before terminating at Cwmaman Colliery Halt. It was built by the Vale of Neath Railway and operated by the GWR from 1865.

78. This photograph from about 1910 was taken near Dare Junction looking west towards Gelli Tarw. The outside framed 0-6-0ST on the left is on the route leading to Bwllfa Dare, whilst the 0-6-0ST on the right is on the Dare & Aman route. Black Lion Crossing would be behind the photographer. (S. Vincent coll.)

BLACK LION CROSSING HALT

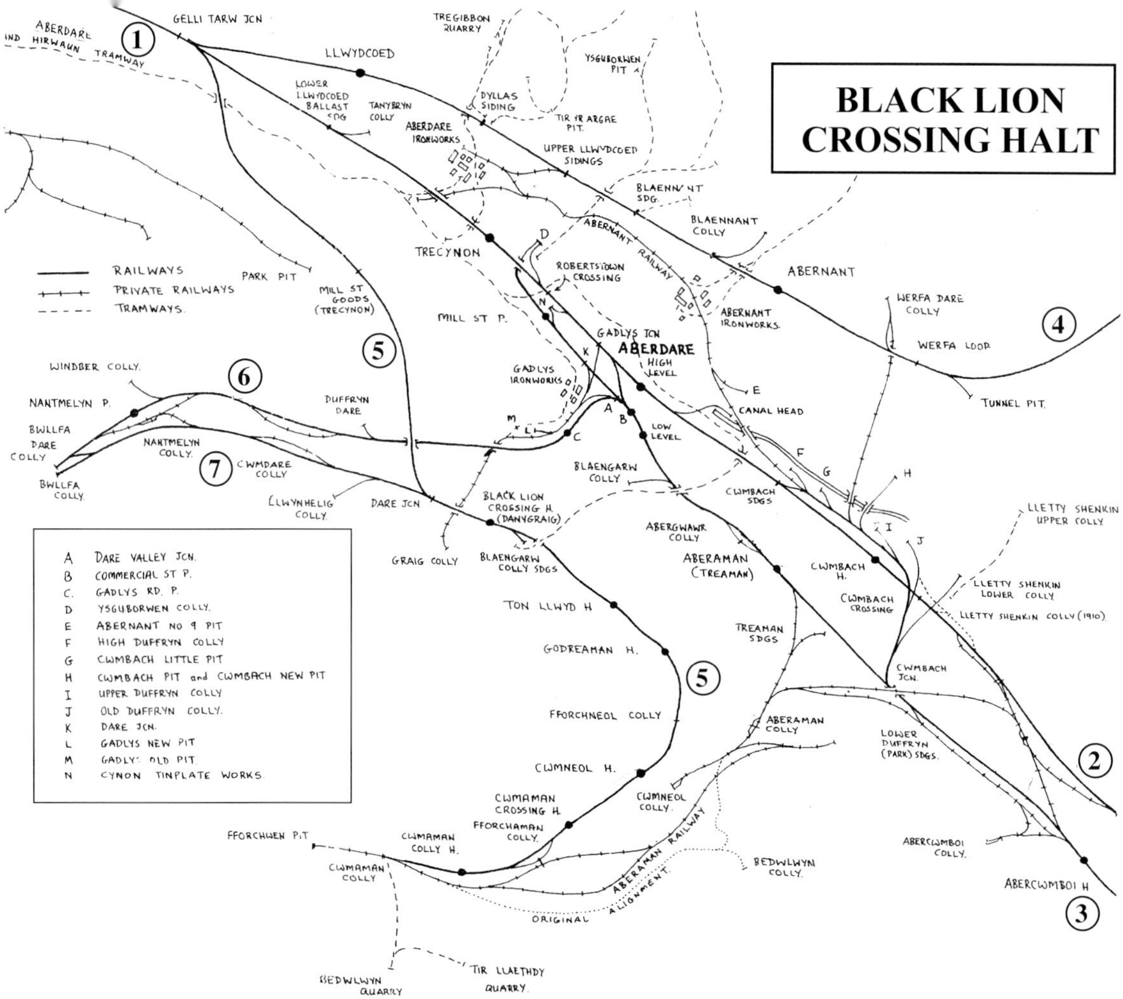

Map key:

- A DARE VALLEY JCN.
- B COMMERCIAL ST P.
- C GADLYS RD. P.
- D YSGUBORWEN COLLY.
- E ABERNANT No 9 PIT
- F HIGH DUFFRYN COLLY
- G CWMBACH LITTLE PIT
- H CWMBACH PIT and CWMBACH NEW PIT
- I UPPER DUFFRYN COLLY
- J OLD DUFFRYN COLLY.
- K DARE JCN.
- L GADLYS NEW PIT
- M GADLYS OLD PIT
- N CYNON TINPLATE WORKS

79. Our unusual journey begins at the short wooden platform forming the northern terminus. Access to the branch was from Gelli Tarw Junction, on the Aberdare to Neath line. A view of the viaduct thereon is to be seen on the back cover. (D.K.Jones coll.)

← XXVIII. This diagram shows the lines at their optimum, with the route names numbered. A line reached Merthyr Dare Colliery in 1854 and a track was laid in the other direction at Dare Junction in 1857, to serve Bwllfa Dare Colliery. The remainder of the Aman branch opened at about that time. The TVR line in the Dare Valley opened in about 1866 and did not carry the public, only workmen. (R.A.Cooke/I.Pope)

1 - To Neath.
2 - To Quakers Yard.
3 - To Abercynon.
4 - To Merthyr.
5 - Dare & Aman Branch (GWR).
6 - Dare Valley Branch (TVR).
7 - Bwllfa Branch (GWR).

XXIX. Moving round the curve, the first halt was Tonllwyd (top left). This 1920 extract makes it clear that the purpose of the route was to serve the residential area. Further south is Godreaman Halt, with empty building plots nearby. Cwmneol Halt was further south, followed by Cwmaman Crossing Halt.

CWMAMAN COLLIERY HALT

80. The southern terminus is featured, with Fforchaman Colliery in the distance. It was completed in 1897 and was eventually linked to Cwmaman Colliery, but not used after 1965. (D.K.Jones coll.)

81. Cwmaman Colliery was sunk in 1849 and closed in 1968. The passenger service on the route operated in 1906-24 only, but the line was open from 1856 until 1936 for freight. Subsequently, the collieries were served by sidings from the east. (D.K.Jones coll.)

6. Aberdare Branch

ABERCYNON NORTH

82. We have already examined Abercynon in detail and picture 23 showed the location of the future North station. It opened on 3rd October 1988, when the 1846 TVR branch reopened. It is seen on the left, from the old island platform, as the 13.30 Merthyr to Penarth runs in on 21st July 1990. (A.C.Hartless)

83. The photographer's son seems puzzled as the 12.25 Barry Island to Aberdare arrives that day. The former engine shed is in the background. Local passengers were often greatly inconvenienced during late running, as there was uncertainty as to which station the next southbound train would arrive at. Caption 24 explains the solution on 18th May 2008, when this structure closed and the suffixes were lost. (A.C.Hartless)

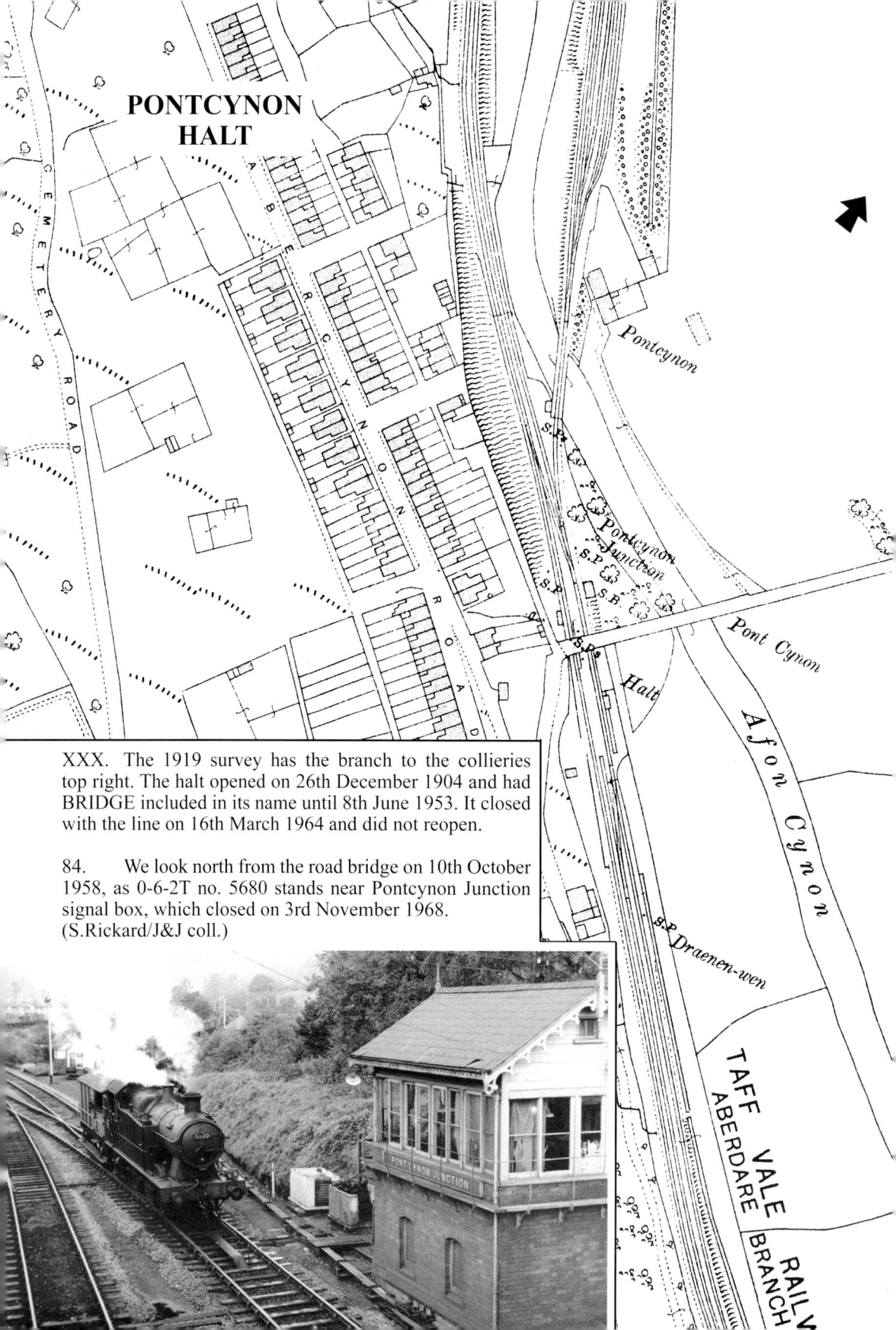

XXX. The 1919 survey has the branch to the collieries top right. The halt opened on 26th December 1904 and had BRIDGE included in its name until 8th June 1953. It closed with the line on 16th March 1964 and did not reopen.

84. We look north from the road bridge on 10th October 1958, as 0-6-2T no. 5680 stands near Pontcynon Junction signal box, which closed on 3rd November 1968. (S.Rickard/J&J coll.)

85. Suburban DMU no. W50122 is working from Aberdare Low Level to Abercynon on 10th October 1958. The bridge over the Afon Cynon is in the background. (S.Rickard/J&J coll.)

86. The other bridge is central in this view from a train on 26th June 1960. It carried Nixon's private railway to the collieries called Cwmcynon (1895-1949), Abergorki (1865-1967), Deep Dyffryn (1850-1979) and Navigation (1878-1991). (M.Dart/ Transport Treasury)

87. The Cynon comes into view on 17th August 1963. The term HALT was added here and at the next stop on 2nd October 1922. (P.J.Garland/R.S.Carpenter)

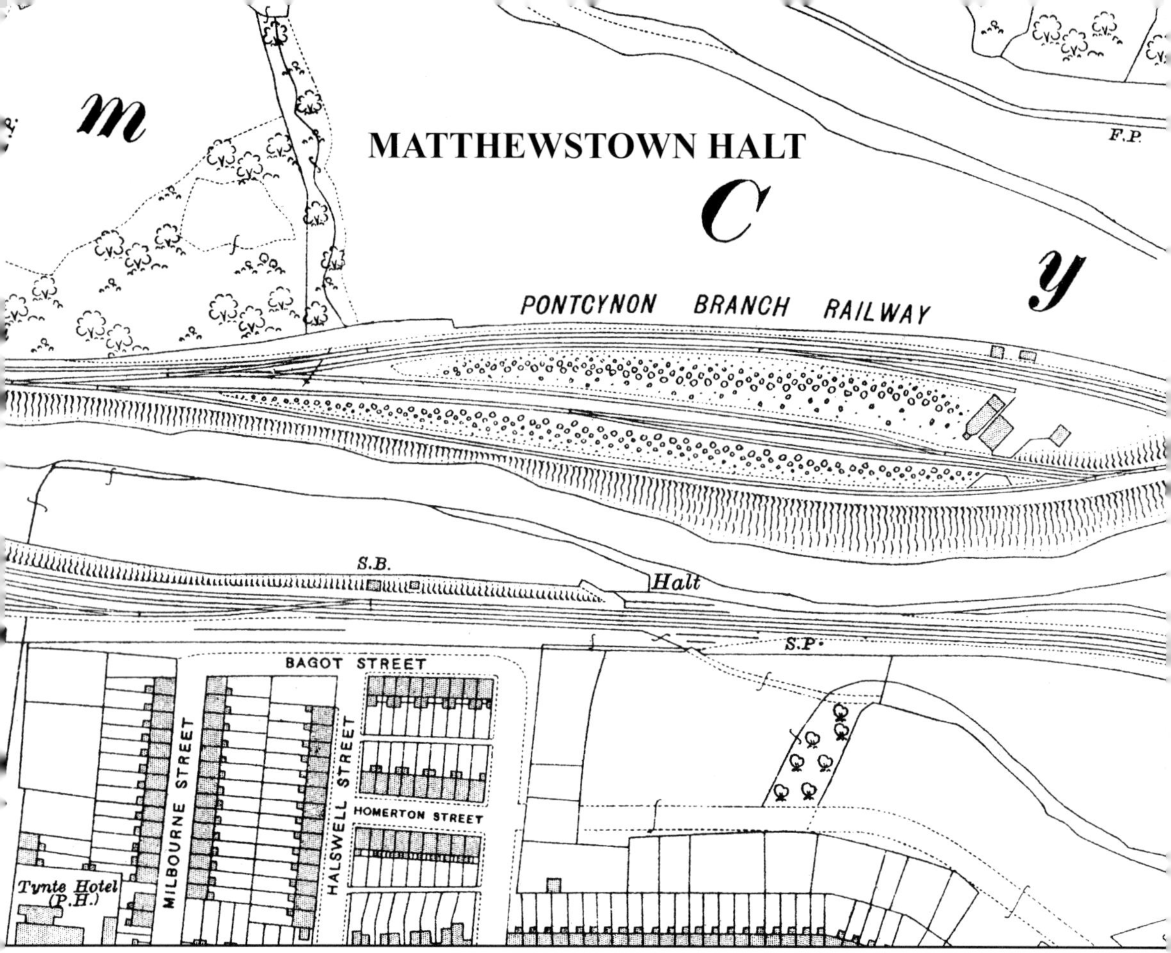

XXXI. The halt opened on 1st October 1914 and is immediately south of the river on this 1919 extract. The colliery lines are north of it.

88. The remnants of the halt were photographed in 1968; it never reopened. Although passenger trains were withdrawn in 1964, there was a heavy freight traffic. In the early 1980s, there were around 30,000 tons carried each way, weekly. No. 37238 is hauling an excursion from Aberdare to the West of England on 14th July 1978. Such trains ceased in 1980, owing to the cost of track maintenance to passenger standards. (P.Jones)

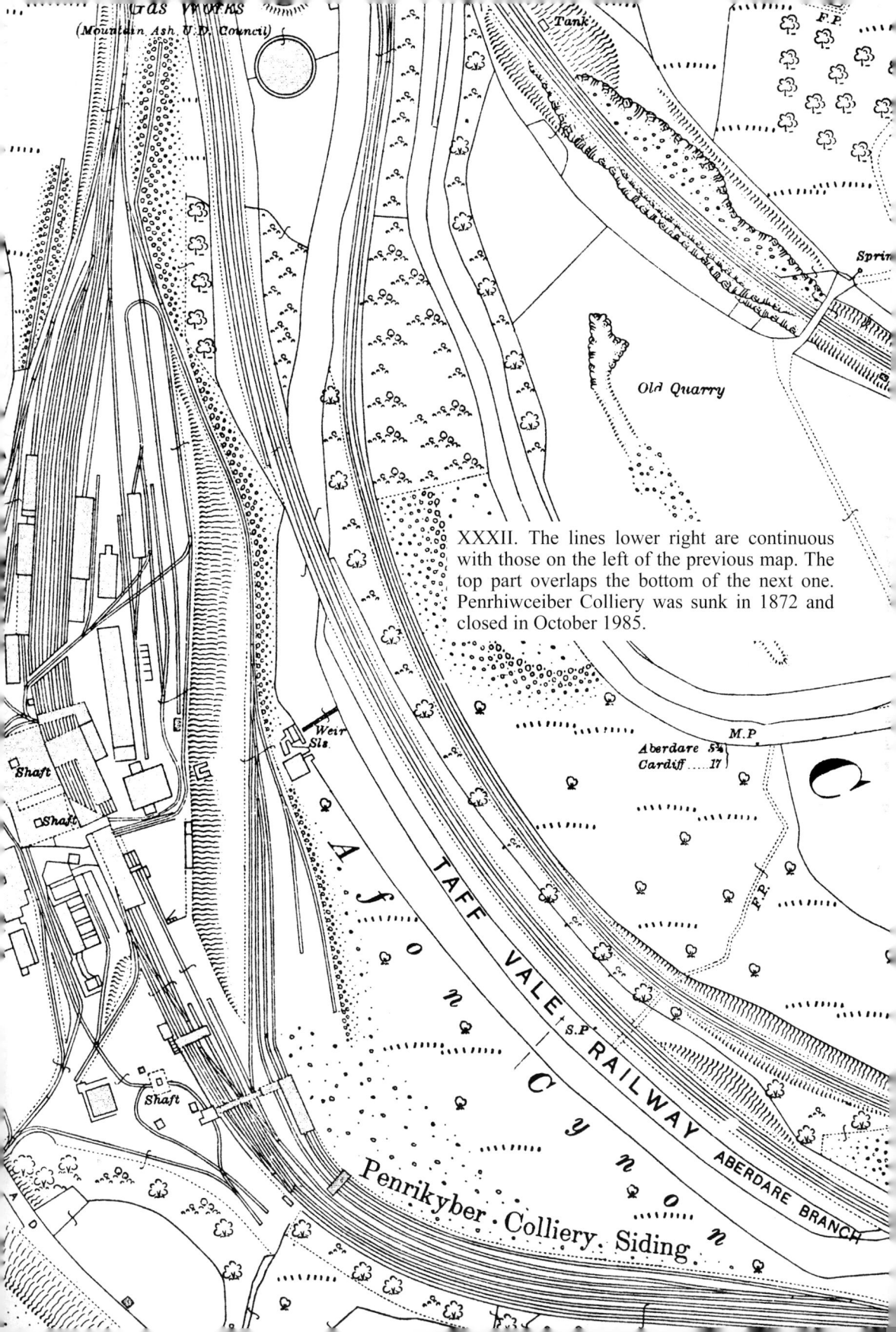

XXXII. The lines lower right are continuous with those on the left of the previous map. The top part overlaps the bottom of the next one. Penrhiwceiber Colliery was sunk in 1872 and closed in October 1985.

PENRHIWCEIBER LOW LEVEL

XXXIII. The TVR station is near the centre of this 1919 survey, while the GWR High Level is right lower. This is illustrated in pictures 111-114 in *Pontypool to Mountain Ash*.

Penrhiwceiber	1923	1923
Passenger tickets issued	74560	28830
Season tickets issued	286	82
Parcels forwarded	15406	11896
General goods forwarded (tons)	231	149
Coal and coke received (tons)	5091	1367
Other minerals received (tons)	4923	1900
General goods received (tons)	49395	27323
Coal and Coke handled	1218038	848813
Trucks of livestock handled -	-	-

89. An indifferent postcard gives the relationship of the TVR station to the GWR, which is in the foreground. (Lens of Sutton Association)

90. The station opened on 1st June 1883 and carried the suffix TVR. This was replaced by LOW LEVEL on 1st July 1924, but neither show here. Note the TVR somersault signal. (Lens of Sutton Association)

91. A view up the valley on 15th July 1959 shows a well groomed station. Just beyond the footbridge is the signal box, which had 24 levers and closed on 3rd November 1968. (H.C.Casserley)

92. A photograph from August 1963 reveals that the station was gaslit to the end. The shadowless lamps are of Suggs' Rochester pattern. (P.J.Garland/R.S.Carpenter)

93. The goods yard was recorded at the same time. It was nearing its end and closed on 2nd December 1963. There were 24 men employed at the station in 1923, but only 17 by 1932. (P.J.Garland/R.S.Carpenter)

94. In contrast to the old station, concrete and steel predominated in the new structure, which opened on 3rd October 1988. However, old chaired track remained and is seen on opening day. (D.K.Jones coll.)

EAST OF MOUNTAIN ASH

95. Nixon's Navigation Colliery is shown, in part, on the right of the next map. Each colliery company had its own fleet of wagons until the advent of World War II. The pit opened in 1895 and employed 1882 men by 1913. It closed in 1949, soon after nationalisation. (A.Dudman coll.)

MOUNTAIN ASH (OXFORD STREET)

96. A westward view in June 1922 has the goods shed on the left and the chimney of Deep Dyffryn Colliery in the distance. The goods yard closed on 2nd December 1963. (D.K.Jones coll.)

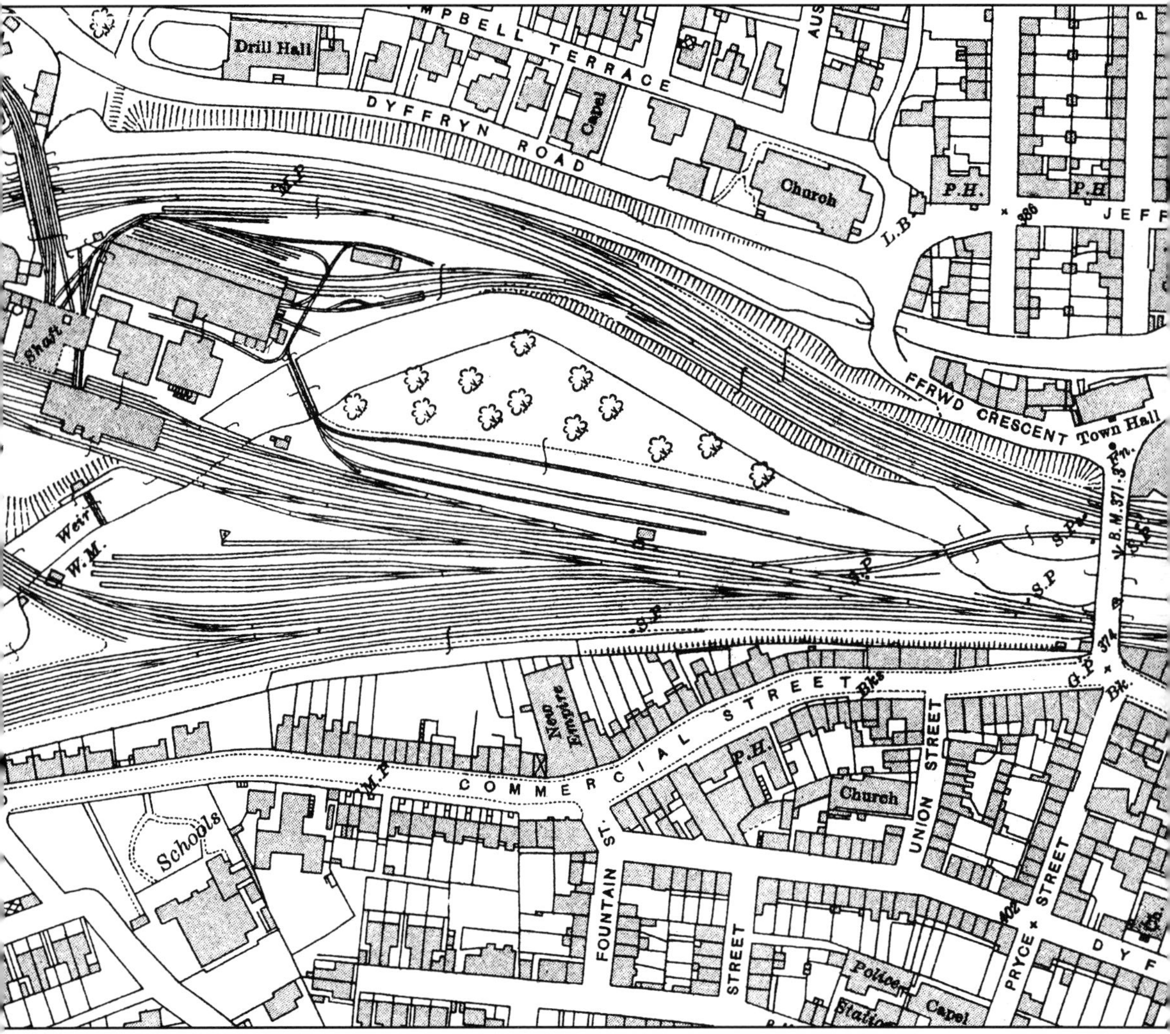

XXXIV. Oxford Street and Cardiff Road are both on the right page and these names were applied to the two nearby stations from 1st July 1924. They were used until both were closed in 1964. This 1919 extract has their earlier initials showing and Deep Dyffryn Colliery on the left. It is interesting

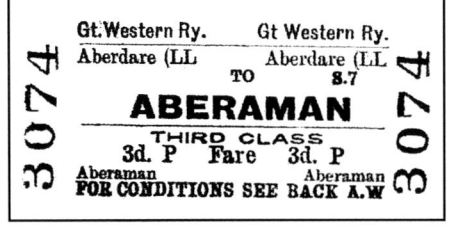

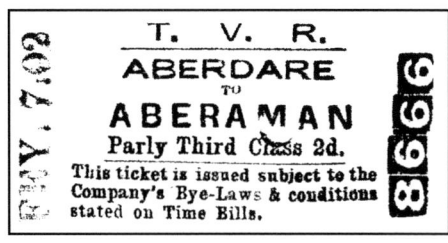

to note the number of lines which cross the river in this short distance. The first TVR station was a little to the right and was in use until 1st January 1857. Lower right is the TVR Nixon's Crossing signal box with, top right, the GWR Cresselly Crossing signal box.

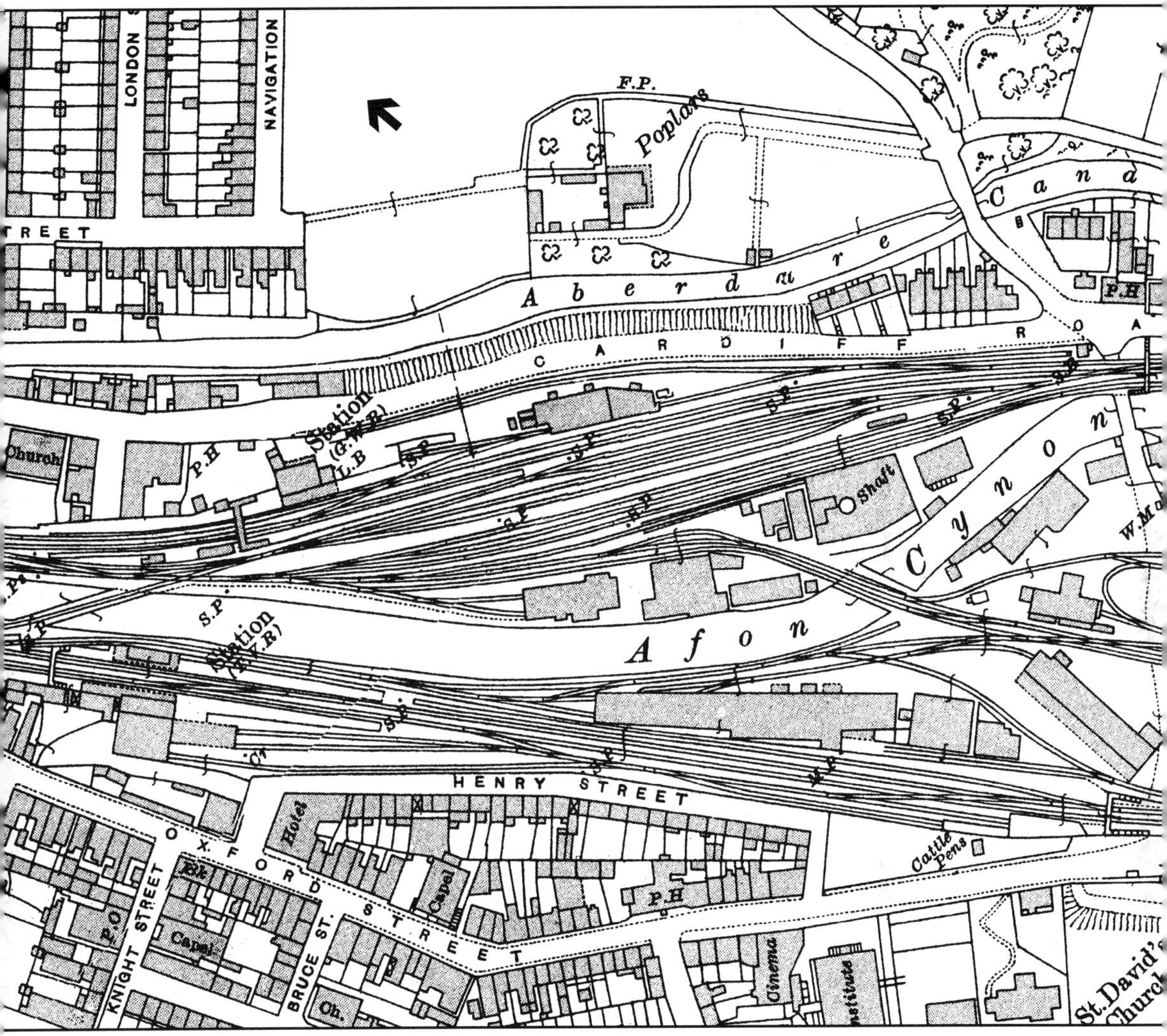

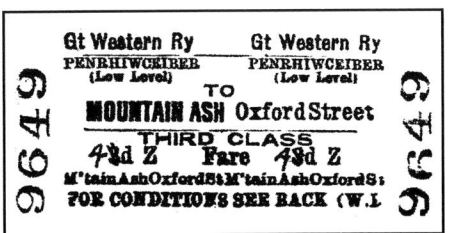

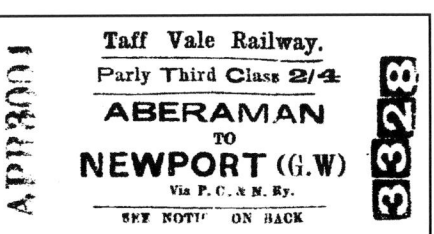

97. The first of five eastward panoramas from the road bridge includes all four platforms; Cardiff Road station is on the left, with its ex-GWR signal box standing high. Other views can be seen in pictures 1 to 6 in *Mountain Ash to Neath*. (D.Lawrence)

98. The signal box had 28 levers and remained in use until 6th September 1964. The river is included in this record from 12th January 1960, as is the siding to the colliery. This mine closed in 1967. (S.Rickard/J&J coll.)

99. Pictured on 23rd May 1973 is Robert Stephenson Hawthorn 0-6-0ST no. 7139 of 1944, working as NCB no. 8. (T.Heavyside)

100. No. 376842 is running up the valley on the newly singled line with a load of coal for processing on 23rd May 1973. The station had a staff of 34 in 1923, but only 20 ten years later. The former down line was then used by the NCB. (T.Heavyside)

101. A rare railtour arrived on 20th October 1979 and is having its rear lamp fitted. It was named the "Deep Duffryn Diddler". (D.H.Mitchell)

MOUNTAIN ASH

102. The new station was a little to the east of the previous one and is seen when new in September 1988. It lasted only 12 years. (D.K.Jones coll.)

103. The replacement station was recorded under construction on 2nd August 2000. The new alignment was for double track. (E.Wilmshurst)

104. The replacement premises came into use on 29th April 2001 and the loop allowed four-car trains to pass. This westward view is from 7th August 2011. (D.K.Jones)

WEST OF MOUNTAIN ASH

105. Our route is diagonally in the lower left corner in this view from 22nd May 1973. No. 8 is seen again, but this time at Deep Dyffryn Colliery. This can be found on the left of the last map; the engine is approaching the Town Hall, across the Cynon. (T.Heavyside)

ABERCWMBOI HALT

Cr XXXV. Opening on 26th December 1904, the halt is marked lower right on the 1919 edition. It came into use as Dyffryn Crossing Platform and became Abercwmboi Platform in 1906 and Halt in 1922. It closed on 2nd April 1956. Top left is Middle Dyffryn Colliery, which ceased to raise coal in 1885 and was used for pumping and ventilation from 1896 instead. It then became the central washery for the area and eventually Phurnacite fuel was manufactured in the area. This explains why loaded trains have been seen running in both directions further down the valley. The briquettes were produced from 1939 from waste small steam coal. 1m tons were produced in the peak year of 1952, but closure came in 1990, ending the dust and smell which were continuous.

106. The minimal facilities were recorded in June 1922, this being the view towards Aberdare. Abercwmboi Colliery was sunk in the 1850s and closed in 1962. (D.K.Jones coll.)

107. The signal box was lower right on the triangular junction and is seen in April 1986. There were 38 levers and they were taken out of use on 9th October 1989. (D.K.Jones coll.)

108. At the Phurnacite Works on 26th May 1973 is no. D6885. The line from a point west of here to Aberdare closed on 29th November 1971. (T.Heavyside)

FERNHILL

109. The new platform was built on the site of Abercwmboi Halt and was opened on 3rd October 1988. No. 143625 is seen from behind as it departs on 12th December 2002, forming the 09.45 Barry Island to Aberdare. (A.C.Hartless)

ABERAMAN

XXXVI. Top left is Abergwawr Colliery, which was sunk in 1854 and after 32 years of operation closed in 1886, when its shaft became an upcast for Aberaman Colliery. The gasworks used waste gases from the Phurnacite plant. The Afon Cynon meanders from top to right across this 1919 map. The station was named Tre-Aman until 26th August 1888. The line lower left leads to Cwmneol, Furchneol, Bedw-Llwyn and Aberaman Collieries. The TVR route from Cwmbach Junction to Aberdare Low Level closed on 29th November 1971, when the link line onto the former GWR Vale of Neath route to Aberdare High Level was reopened.

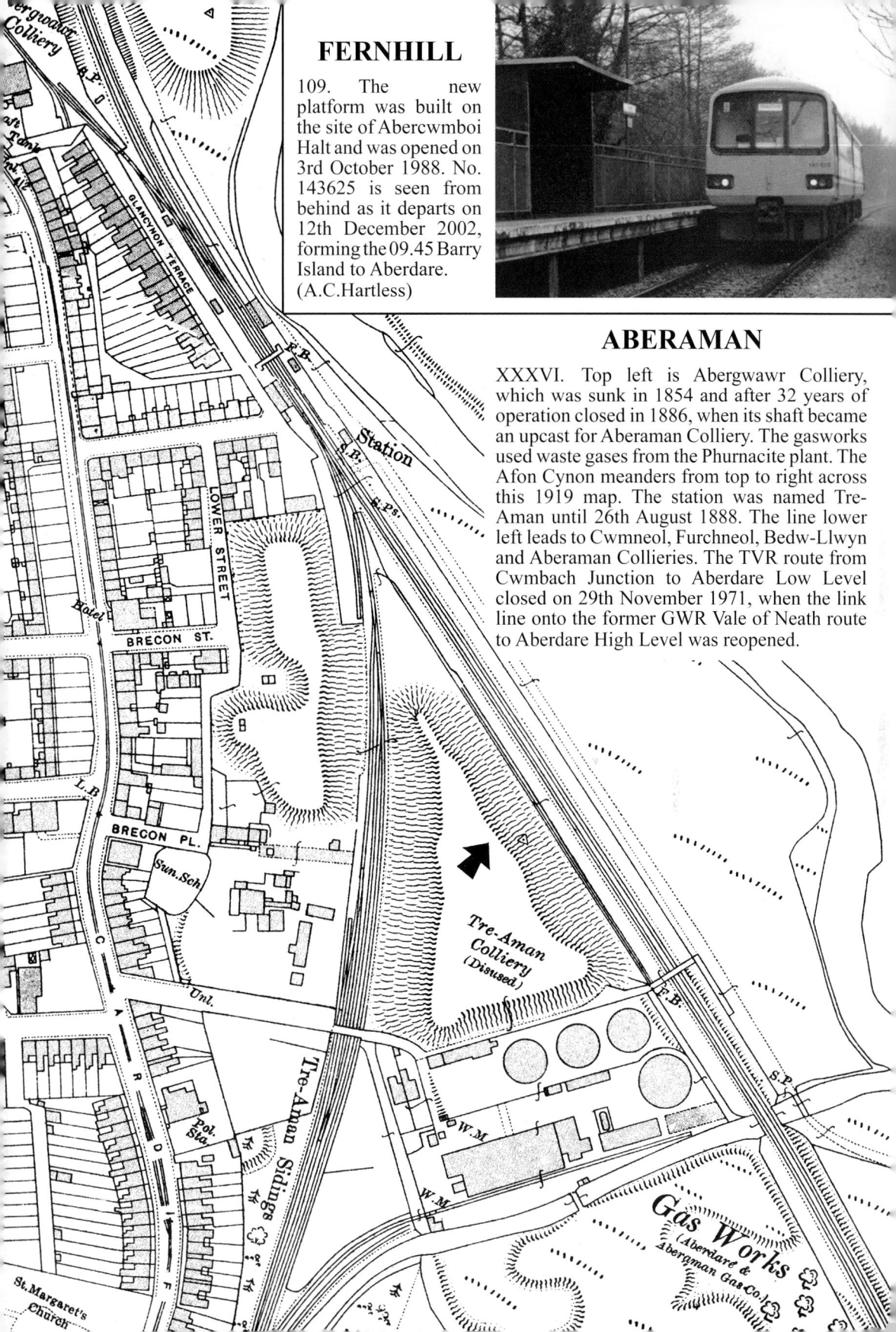

110. This classic postcard image has Tre-Aman sidings diverging lower left. The box had 22 levers and lasted until 6th October 1967, having opened in 1912. The staff numbered 17 in 1923 and 12 in 1936. (Lens of Sutton Association)

111. A southward view on 17th August 1963 features a waste tip and a gas holder, plus the opportunity for a trip to Bristol for 16/9d. A passing loop was retained after the route was reopened to passengers, the entire branch being controlled from Abercynon.
(P.J.Garland/R.S.Carpenter)

Aberaman	1923	1933
Passenger tickets issued	51572	47783
Season tickets issued	204	147
Parcels forwarded	18484	25619
General goods forwarded (tons)	33	11
Coal and coke received (tons)	43	1169
Other minerals received (tons)	275	252
General goods received (tons)	1250	18790
Coal and Coke handled	183842	408541
Trucks of livestock handled	-	-

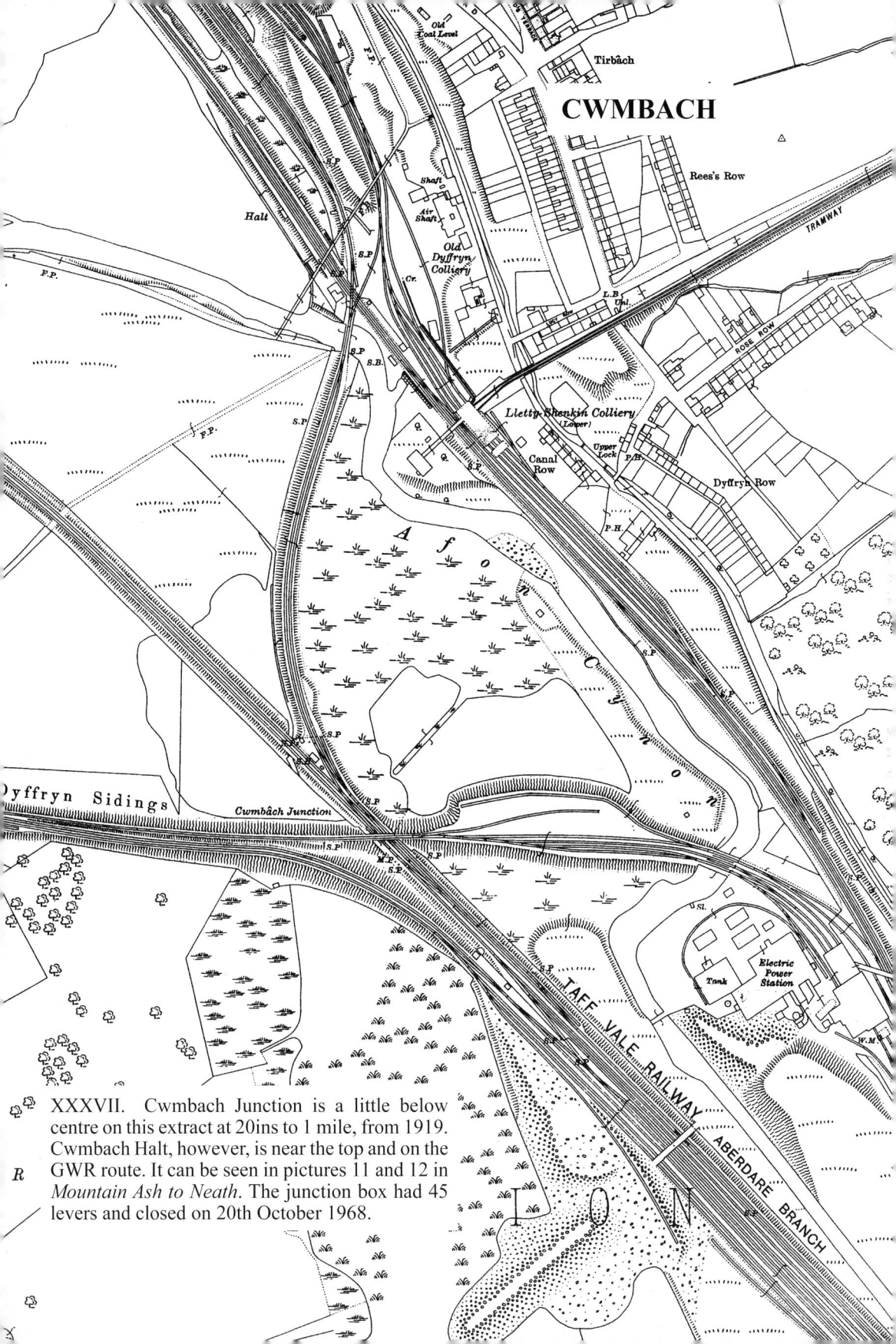

XXXVII. Cwmbach Junction is a little below centre on this extract at 20ins to 1 mile, from 1919. Cwmbach Halt, however, is near the top and on the GWR route. It can be seen in pictures 11 and 12 in *Mountain Ash to Neath*. The junction box had 45 levers and closed on 20th October 1968.

112. Prior to the reopening in 1988, a connection was made between the earlier TVR and GWR routes, as the former was needed for a new road. A fresh bridge over the river was required and this came from Wheatley, between Princes Risborough and Oxford. No. 143613 is working the 14.20 Aberdare to Barry Island service on 1st March 1998, this being the rear of it. (A.C.Hartless)

113. The new Cwmbach platform was built on the old GWR alignment, much closer to the community, and on the north side of the line. The same train is about to stop. All platforms were built for five coaches in 1988. The line was slewed in 1973. (A.C.Hartless)

ABERDARE LOW LEVEL

XXXVIII. The 1920 edition has the TVR terminus left of centre and the GWR's through station at the top. The river is close to the former route. The goods yard crane (Cr.) was rated at 3-tons. The suffix was used from 1st July 1924.

Views of Aberdare High Level can be seen in pictures 15 to 34 in *Mountain Ash to Neath*.

114. The map reveals that the platform canopy was very long. This is its southern end in 1922, with the goods shed entrance on the left. The roof of the locomotive shed is on the right. There had been 21 private sidings nearby in 1938. (D.K.Jones coll.)

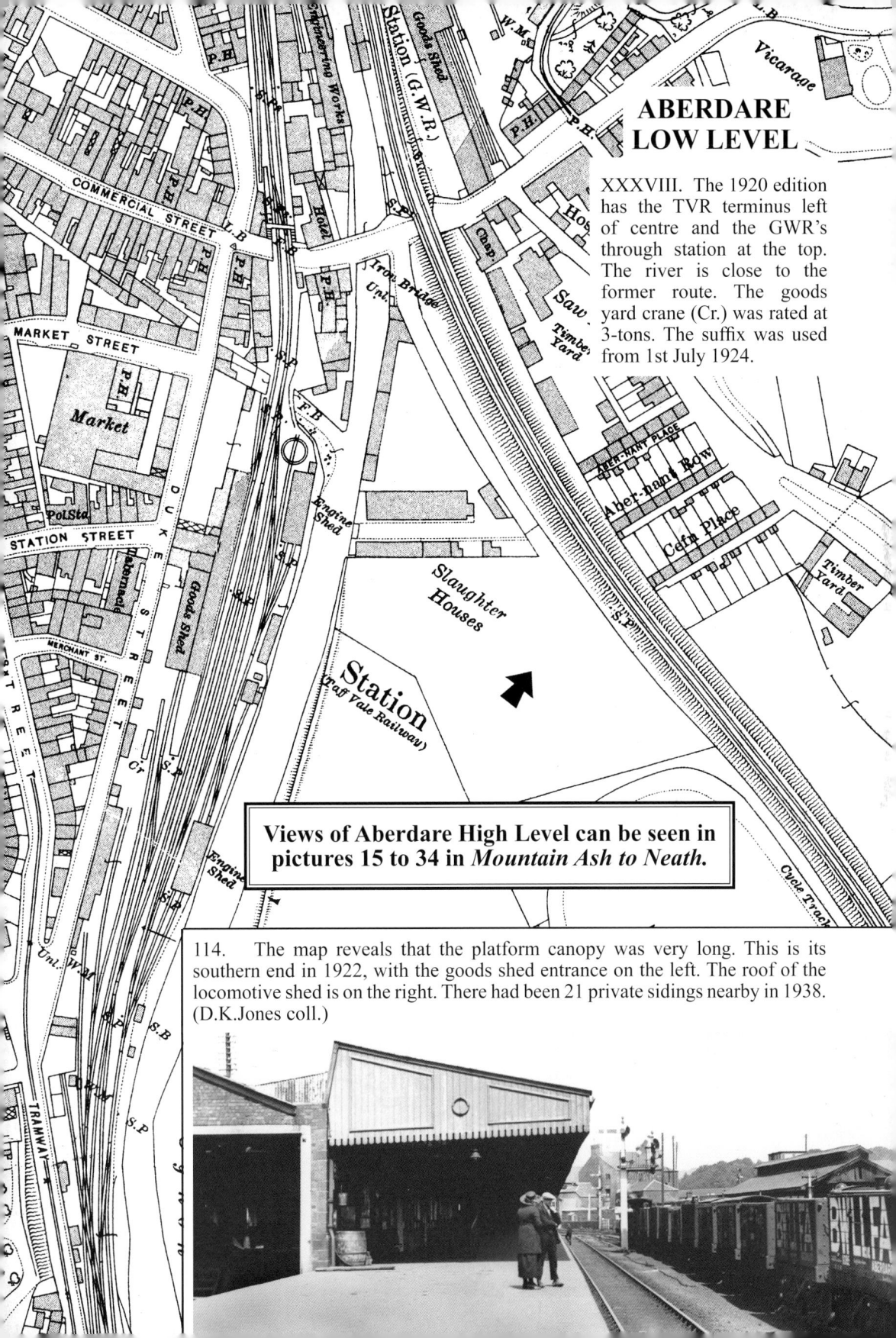

115. The engine shed is on the left of this 1956 view. It was in use from 1865 to 1927, when the GWR one at High Level sufficed. The van shows ROYAL but not MAIL.
(R.M.Casserley)

116. This is the passenger's perspective from Duke Street in 1956, not enhanced by the low brick wall. The buildings were demolished in 1968. The staff had numbered 79 in 1923 and was down to 41 by 1935.
(R.M.Casserley)

117. At the north end of the station area was Commercial Street level crossing and adjacent to it was a footbridge from which this photograph was taken in January 1960. In the distance is Dare Valley Junction from which the 1866 line curved left to that place.
(D.K.Jones coll.)

118. A southward panorama on 17th August 1963 records South Box. Its 54-lever frame was in use until 13th December 1964, although passenger service had ceased on 16th March and freight likewise on 3rd August of that year. (P.J.Garland/R.S.Carpenter)

119. A northward view on the same day includes North Box and the buffer stops of the platform road. The box had 49 levers and functioned until 30th July 1973. A DMU waits on the right. Further north, there had been stops at Commercial Street Platform and Mill Street Platform for the public from 26th November 1904 until 1st June 1912. The latter was also open from 5th April 1847 to 21st November 1852 and was then the TVR terminus. (P.J.Garland/R.S.Carpenter)

ABERDARE

120. As explained, the TVR trackbed was needed for highway improvements and so the ex-GWR line was brought back into passenger use. A new platform was built on the site of the down one at High Level. The breezy location is seen on 23rd March 2006 with a train terminating from Barry Island. Freight continued to Hirwaun again from January 1998. (V.Mitchell)

Middleton Press
EVOLVING THE ULTIMATE RAIL ENCYCLOPEDIA

Easebourne Lane, Midhurst, West Sussex.
GU29 9AZ Tel:01730 813169
www.middletonpress.co.uk email:info@middletonpress.co.uk
A-978 0 906520 B- 978 1 873793 C- 978 1 901706 D-978 1 904474
E - 978 1 906008 F - 978 1 908174

All titles listed below were in print at time of publication - please check current availability by looking at our website - *www.middletonpress.co.uk* or by requesting a Brochure which includes our LATEST RAILWAY TITLES also our TRAMWAY, TROLLEYBUS, MILITARY and WATERWAYS series

A
Abergavenny to Merthyr C 91 8
Abertillery and Ebbw Vale Lines D 84 5
Aberystwyth to Carmarthen E 90 1
Allhallows - Branch Line to A 62 8
Alton - Branch Lines to A 11 6
Andover to Southampton A 82 6
Ascot - Branch Lines around A 64 2
Ashburton - Branch Line to B 95 4
Ashford - Steam to Eurostar B 67 1
Ashford to Dover A 48 2
Austrian Narrow Gauge D 04 3
Avonmouth - BL around D 42 5
Aylesbury to Rugby D 91 3

B
Baker Street to Uxbridge D 90 6
Bala to Llandudno E 87 1
Banbury to Birmingham D 27 2
Banbury to Cheltenham E 63 5
Bangor to Holyhead F 01 7
Bangor to Portmadoc E 72 7
Barking to Southend C 80 2
Barmouth to Pwllheli E 53 6
Barry - Branch Lines around D 50 0
Bath Green Park to Bristol C 36 9
Bath to Evercreech Junction A 60 4
Beamish 40 years on rails E94 9
Bedford to Wellingborough D 31 9
Birmingham to Wolverhampton E253
Bletchley to Cambridge D 94 4
Bletchley to Rugby E 07 9
Bodmin - Branch Lines around B 83 1
Bournemouth to Evercreech Jn A 46 8
Bournemouth to Weymouth A 57 4
Bradshaws Guide 1866 F 05 5
Bradshaws Rail Times 1850 F 13 0
Bradshaws Rail Times 1895 F 11 6
Branch Lines series - see town names
Brecon to Neath D 43 2
Brecon to Newport D 16 6
Brecon to Newtown E 06 2
Brighton to Eastbourne A 16 1
Brighton to Worthing A 03 1
Bromley South to Rochester B 23 7
Bromsgrove to Birmingham D 87 6
Bromsgrove to Gloucester D 73 9
Brunel - A railtour D 74 6
Bude - Branch Line to B 29 9
Burnham to Evercreech Jn B 68 0

C
Cambridge to Ely D 55 5
Canterbury - BLs around B 58 9
Cardiff to Dowlais (Cae Harris) E 47 5
Cardiff to Pontypridd E 95 6
Cardiff to Swansea E 42 0
Carlisle to Hawick E 85 7
Carmarthen to Fishguard E 66 6
Caterham & Tattenham Corner B251
Central & Southern Spain NG E 91 8
Chard and Yeovil - BLs a C 30 7
Charing Cross to Dartford A 75 8
Charing Cross to Orpington A 96 3
Cheddar - Branch Line to B 90 9
Cheltenham to Andover C 43 7
Cheltenham to Redditch D 81 4
Chester to Rhyl E 93 2
Chichester to Portsmouth A 14 7
Clacton and Walton - BLs to F 04 8
Clapham Jn to Beckenham Jn B 36 7
Cleobury Mortimer - BLs a E 18 5
Clevedon & Portishead - BLs to D180

Colonel Stephens - His Empire D 62 3
Consett to South Shields E 57 4
Cornwall Narrow Gauge D 56 2
Corris and Vale of Rheidol E 65 9
Craven Arms to Llandeilo E 35 2
Craven Arms to Wellington E 33 8
Crawley to Littlehampton A 34 5
Cromer - Branch Lines around C 26 0
Croydon to East Grinstead B 48 0
Crystal Palace & Catford Loop B 87 1
Cyprus Narrow Gauge E 13 0

D
Darjeeling Revisited F 09 3
Darlington Leamside Newcastle E 28 4
Darlington to Newcastle D 98 2
Dartford to Sittingbourne B 34 3
Derwent Valley - BL to the D 06 7
Devon Narrow Gauge E 09 3
Didcot to Banbury D 02 9
Didcot to Swindon C 84 0
Didcot to Winchester C 13 0
Dorset & Somerset NG D 76 0
Douglas - Laxey - Ramsey E 75 8
Douglas to Peel C 88 8
Douglas to Port Erin C 55 0
Douglas to Ramsey D 39 5
Dover to Ramsgate A 78 9
Dublin Northwards in 1950s E 31 4
Dunstable - Branch Lines to E 27 7

E
Ealing to Slough C 42 0
East Cornwall Mineral Railways D 22 7
East Croydon to Three Bridges A 53 6
Eastern Spain Narrow Gauge E 56 7
East Grinstead - BLs to A 07 9
East London - Branch Lines of C 44 4
East London Line B 80 0
East of Norwich - Branch Lines E 69 7
Effingham Junction - BLs a A 74 1
Ely to Norwich C 90 1
Enfield Town & Palace Gates D 32 6
Epsom to Horsham A 30 7
Eritrean Narrow Gauge E 38 3
Euston to Harrow & Wealdstone C 89 5
Exeter to Barnstaple B 15 2
Exeter to Newton Abbot C 49 9
Exeter to Tavistock B 69 5
Exmouth - Branch Lines B 00 8

F
Fairford - Branch Line to A 52 9
Falmouth, Helston & St. Ives C 74 1
Fareham to Salisbury A 67 3
Faversham to Dover B 05 3
Felixstowe & Aldeburgh - BL to D 20 3
Fenchurch Street to Barking C 20 8
Festiniog - 50 yrs of enterprise C 83 3
Festiniog 1946-55 E 01 7
Festiniog in the Fifties B 68 8
Festiniog in the Sixties B 91 6
Finsbury Park to Alexandra Pal C 02 8
Frome to Bristol B 77 0

G
Gloucester to Bristol D 35 7
Gloucester to Cardiff D 66 1
Gosport - Branch Lines around A 36 9
Greece Narrow Gauge D 72 2

H
Hampshire Narrow Gauge D 36 4
Harrow to Watford D 14 2
Harwich & Hadleigh - BLs to F 02 4
Hastings to Ashford A 37 6

Hawkhurst - Branch Line to A 66 6
Hayling - Branch Line to A 12 3
Hay-on-Wye - BL around D 92 0
Haywards Heath to Seaford A 28 4
Hemel Hempstead - BLs to D 88 3
Henley, Windsor & Marlow C77 2
Hereford to Newport D 54 8
Hertford & Hatfield - BLs a E 58 1
Hertford Loop E 71 0
Hexham to Carlisle D 75 3
Hexham to Hawick F 08 6
Hitchin to Peterborough D 07 4
Holborn Viaduct to Lewisham A 81 9
Horsham - Branch Lines to A 02 4
Huntingdon - Branch Line to A 93 2

I
Ilford to Shenfield C 97 0
Ilfracombe - Branch Line to B 21 3
Industrial Rlys of the South East A 09 3
Ipswich to Saxmundham C 41 3
Isle of Wight Lines - 50 yrs C 12 3

K
Kent Narrow Gauge C 45 1
Kidderminster to Shrewsbury E 10 9
Kingsbridge - Branch Line to C 98 7
Kings Cross to Potters Bar E 62 8
Kingston & Hounslow Loops A 83 3
Kingswear - Branch Line to C 17 8

L
Lambourn - Branch Line to C 70 3
Launceston & Princetown C 19 2
Lewisham to Dartford A 92 5
Lines around Wimbledon B 75 6
Liverpool Street to Chingford D 01 2
Liverpool Street to Ilford C 34 5
Llandeilo to Swansea E 46 8
London Bridge to Addiscombe B 20 6
London Bridge to East Croydon A 58 1
Longmoor - Branch Lines to A 41 3
Looe - Branch Line to C 22 2
Lowestoft - BLs around E 40 6
Ludlow to Hereford E 14 7
Lydney - Branch Lines around E 26 0
Lyme Regis - Branch Line to A 45 1
Lynton - Branch Line to B 04 6

M
Machynlleth to Barmouth E 54 3
Maesteg and Tondu Lines E 06 2
March - Branch Lines around B 09 1
Marylebone to Rickmansworth D 49 4
Melton Constable to Yarmouth Bch E031
Midhurst - Branch Lines of E 78 9
Mitcham Junction Lines B 01 5
Mitchell & company C 59 8
Monmouth - Branch Lines to E 20 8
Monmouthshire Eastern Valleys D 71 5
Moretonhampstead - BL to C 27 7
Moreton-in-Marsh to Worcester D 26 5
Mountain Ash to Neath D 80 7

N
Newbury to Westbury C 66 6
Newcastle to Hexham D 69 2
Newport (IOW) - Branch Lines to A 26 0
Newquay - Branch Lines to C 71 0
Newton Abbot to Plymouth C 60 4
Newtown to Aberystwyth E 41 3
North East German NG D 44 9
Northern France Narrow Gauge C 75 8
Northern Spain Narrow Gauge E 83 3
North London Line B 94 7
North Woolwich - BLs around C 65 9

O
Ongar - Branch Line to E 05 5
Oswestry - Branch Lines around E 60 4
Oswestry to Whitchurch E 81 9
Oxford to Bletchley D 57 9
Oxford to Moreton-in-Marsh D 15 9

P
Paddington to Ealing C 37 6
Paddington to Princes Risborough C819
Padstow - Branch Line to B 54 1
Peterborough to Kings Lynn E 32 1
Plymouth - BLs around B 98 5
Plymouth to St. Austell C 63 5
Pontypool to Mountain Ash D 65 4
Pontypridd to Merthyr F 14 7
Pontypridd to Port Talbot E 86 4
Porthmadog 1954-94 - BL a B 31 2
Portmadoc 1923-46 - BLa a B 13 8
Portsmouth to Southampton A 31 4
Portugal Narrow Gauge E 67 3
Potters Bar to Cambridge D 70 8
Princes Risborough - BL to D 05 0
Princes Risborough to Banbury C 85 7

R
Reading to Basingstoke B 27 5
Reading to Didcot C 79 6
Reading to Guildford A 47 5
Redhill to Ashford A 73 4
Return to Blaenau 1970-82 C 64 2
Rhymney & New Tredegar Lines E 48 2
Rickmansworth to Aylesbury D 61 6
Romania & Bulgaria NG E 23 9
Romneyrail C 32 1
Ross-on-Wye - BLs around E 30 7
Ruabon to Barmouth E 84 0
Rugby to Birmingham E 37 6
Rugby to Loughborough F 12 3
Rugby to Stafford F 07 9
Ryde to Ventnor A 19 2

S
Salisbury to Westbury B 39 8
Saxmundham to Yarmouth C 69 7
Saxony Narrow Gauge D 47 0
Seaton & Sidmouth - BLs to A 95 6
Selsey - Branch Line to A 04 8
Sheerness - Branch Line to B 16 2
Shenfield to Ipswich E 96 3
Shrewsbury - Branch Line to A 86 4
Shrewsbury to Chester E 70 3
Shrewsbury to Ludlow E 21 5
Shrewsbury to Newtown E 29 1
Sierra Leone Narrow Gauge D 28 9
Sirhowy Valley Line E 12 3
Sittingbourne to Ramsgate A 90 1
Slough to Newbury C 56 7
South African Two-foot gauge E 51 2
Southampton to Bournemouth A 42 0
Southend & Southminster BLs E 76 5
Southern France Narrow Gauge C 47 5
South London Line B 46 6
South Lynn to Norwich City F 03 1
Southwold - Branch Line to A 15 4
Spalding - Branch Lines around E 52 9
St Albans to Bedford D 08 1
St. Austell to Penzance C 67 3
Steaming through West Hants A 69 7
Stourbridge to Wolverhampton E 16 1
St. Pancras to Barking D 68 5
St. Pancras to Folkestone E 88 8
St. Pancras to St. Albans C 78 9
Stratford-u-Avon to Birmingham D777

Stratford-u-Avon to Cheltenha
ST the Isle of Wight A 56 7
Surrey Narrow Gauge C 87 1
Sussex Narrow Gauge C 68 0
Swanley to Ashford B 45 9
Swansea to Carmarthen E 59
Swindon to Bristol C 96 3
Swindon to Gloucester D 46 3
Swindon to Newport D 30 2
Swiss Narrow Gauge C 94 9

T
Talyllyn 60 E 98 7
Taunton to Barnstaple B 60 2
Taunton to Exeter C 82 6
Tavistock to Plymouth B 88 6
Tenterden - Branch Line to A
Three Bridges to Brighton A 3
Tilbury Loop C 86 4
Tiverton - BLS a C 62 8
Tivetshall to Beccles D 41 8
Tonbridge to Hastings A 44 4
Torrington - Branch Lines to
Towcester - BLs around E 39
Tunbridge Wells BLs A 32 1

U
Upwell - Branch Line to B 64

V
Victoria to Bromley South A 9
Vivarais Revisited E 08 6

W
Wantage - Branch Line to D 2
Wareham to Swanage 50 yrs
Waterloo to Windsor A 54 3
Waterloo to Woking A 38 3
Watford to Leighton Buzzard
Welshpool to Llanfair E 49 9
Wenford Bridge to Fowey C 0
Westbury to Bath B 55 8
Westbury to Taunton C 76 5
West Cornwall Mineral Rlys D
West Croydon to Epsom B 08
West German Narrow Gauge
West London - BLs of C 50 5
West London Line B 84 8
West Wiltshire - BLs of D 12
Weymouth - Woking A 65 9
Willesden Jn to Richmond B
Wimbledon to Beckenham C
Wimbledon to Epsom B 62 6
Wimborne - BLs around A 97
Wisbech - BLs a C 01 7
Witham & Kelvedon - BLs a E
Woking to Alton A 59 8
Woking to Portsmouth A 25 3
Woking to Southampton A 55
Wolverhampton to Shrewsbu
Worcester to Birmingham D 9
Worcester to Hereford D 38 8
Worthing to Chichester A 06

Y
Yeovil - 50 yrs change C 38 3
Yeovil to Dorchester A 76 5
Yeovil to Exeter A 91 8

96